the travel tips

Suzi Rainone

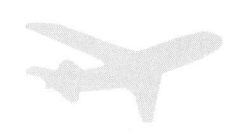

Penguin Books

Penguin Books

Published by the Penguin Group
Penguin Books Australia Ltd
250 Camberwell Road, Camberwell, Victoria 3124, Australia
Penguin Books Ltd
80 Strand, London WC2R 0RL, England
Penguin Putnam Inc.
375 Hudson Street, New York, New York 10014, USA
Penguin Books, a division of Pearson Canada
10 Alcorn Avenue, Toronto, Ontario, Canada M4V 3B2
Penguin Books (NZ) Ltd
Cnr Rosedale and Airborne Roads, Albany, Auckland, New Zealand
Penguin Books (South Africa) (Pty) Ltd
24 Sturdee Avenue, Rosebank, Johannesburg 2196, South Africa
Penguin Books India (P) Ltd
11, Community Centre, Panchsheel Park, New Delhi 110 017, India

First published by Penguin Books Australia Ltd 2003

10 9 8 7 6 5 4 3 2

Copyright © Penguin Books Australia Ltd 2003

All rights reserved. Without limiting the rights under copyright reserved above, no part of this publication may be reproduced, stored in or introduced into a retrieval system, or transmitted, in any form or by any means (electronic, mechanical, photocopying, recording or otherwise), without the prior written permission of both the copyright owner and the above publisher of this book.

Cover design and illustrations by Irma Schick, Penguin Design Studio
Text design by Louise Leffler, Penguin Design Studio
Typeset in 10/15 pt Sabon by Midland Typesetters,
Maryborough, Victoria
Printed and bound in Australia by McPherson's Printing Group,
Maryborough, Victoria

National Library of Australia
Cataloguing-in-Publication data:

Rainone, Suzi.
  The Penguin pocket book of travel tips.

  ISBN 0 14 300060 8.

  1. Travel – Guidebooks. I. Title (Series: Penguin pocket series).

910.202

www.penguin.com.au

contents

	INTRODUCTION	ix
1	**GETTING GOING**	
	Go solo or with company?	1
	Deciding on a destination	5
	Planning an itinerary	13
	Gathering local contacts	15
2	**TICKET TO RIDE**	
	Getting the best fare	16
	Countries with cheap fares	20
	Taking out travel insurance	22
3	**TRAVEL DOCUMENTS AND MONEY**	
	Passports	25
	Visas	26
	Working overseas	31
	Traveller's cheques versus cards	35
	Negotiating fluctuating exchange rates	36
	Having a back-up	40
	Wills and power of attorney	41
4	**HEALTH**	
	Insurance	43

vi CONTENTS

Vaccinations	44
Getting in shape before you go	45
Travelling with medication	47
Packing a medical kit	47
Water and food	50
Recovering from common ailments	52

5 TRAVEL GUIDES

What's on the market	58

6 PACKING

Choosing the right luggage	69
Don't leave home without . . .	73
Packing light	75

7 SAFETY

Keeping travel documents and money safe	81
What to do in a legal emergency	89
Hitchhiking	92
Women travelling alone	94
Sexual harassment	98
Gay and lesbian travellers	100

8 FLYING

Flying after 11 September	102
Surviving long-distance flights	103

CONTENTS **vii**

Travel sickness	109
Lost luggage	110
Staying sane during flight delays	112

9 ON ARRIVAL

Orientating yourself at your destination	113
Changing money	115
Dealing with culture shock	117
Acclimatising	119
Meeting locals and other travellers	121
Making the most of your time and location	122

10 CULTURAL PROTOCOL

General tips on cultural issues	125
Dealing with the police	130
Toilets around the world	131

11 PLANNING YOUR DAYS

When your time away is limited	135

12 LANGUAGE

Making yourself understood	139
Learning a bit before you go	140
Language courses overseas	143

13 TRANSPORT

Negotiating local transport	145
Travel passes	151

14 ACCOMMODATION

Pre-booking a place	156
Finding a place on arrival	158
What to look for	161

15 SHOPPING

What you can bring back to Australia	167
Sending bulky things home	168
Bargaining	169
If you've been ripped off	170

16 TRAVELLING WITH OTHERS

Groups	172
Organised tours	173
Children	175
TOP TEN TRAVEL TIPS	179

introduction

How many times have you farewelled friends at the airport, gazed wistfully at the destinations on the departure board and thought, 'I could be there in a day'? Jetting off with just a ticket in hand may seem adventurous and romantic, but successful and happy travel requires a degree of planning. You don't want to glean some fascinating historical tidbit about your destination just as you're leaving. Nor do you want to over-plan your trip, so that your schedule becomes oppressive – a shopping list of attractions to tick off.

The tips in this book are points for independent travellers to consider before and during a trip. Not all may be relevant to your travels; nor is this an exhaustive checklist. But doing some homework about the mechanics of travel and knowing something of what to expect when you arrive helps you make the most of your time and hard-earned money, and enhances your enjoyment of the trip.

Happy trails.

chapter 1: GETTING GOING

Go solo or with company?

This could be the most important decision of your trip. Travelling solo means blessed freedom to do whatever you want, whenever you want. There's time for reflection and appreciation, to linger longer over that Rembrandt in the Rijksmuseum. Travelling alone makes you more open to meeting new people, whereas groups tend to be self-contained, and couples usually seek out other couples.

But travelling solo also means there's no one to share the many costs – for hotel rooms, taxis and hire cars – or to help with the chores: laundry, shopping, cooking and driving. And there's no one to mind the bags while you duck into the toilet. Personal safety can be a bigger consideration if you travel alone, especially if you're a woman. A table for one often isn't much fun, and some eating establishments may turn down lone diners in favour of bigger-spending couples. Apart from discrimination, solo travellers in some places are objects of pity or intense curiosity. Expect to draw attention.

Long hauls in difficult destinations can sorely test the self-reliance of the solo traveller. There's no one to bounce ideas off. Does this street look safe? Is this food okay? Taking in the world's great monuments, artworks and natural wonders can be a lonely exercise without another person's company and feedback.

Your age and experience, as well as the destination and type of trip, are all points to consider in deciding whether to go it alone. A Hawaiian beach holiday poses few challenges for the travel novice. Backpacking in Western and central Europe is also safe and familiar territory. But if Dhaka is the destination of your first overseas trip, you could be overwhelmed.

Travelling with others brings a mixture of conflicts and rewards. Your best friend may be a living saint but it doesn't mean you share their idea of holiday heaven. You could be surprised at the airport when you check-in your dusty backpack and your friend pulls up with a pile of Louis Vuitton. If you both yearn to go to India, ask each other what you hope to see and do there. Plan some individual time and activities on the trip; don't spend every waking hour together. Before the big event, consider a couple of test-run weekends away.

Also, know thyself. Don't get talked into hiking in the Himalayas by a friend if your vacation nirvana is Venice. If, on the other hand, you're happy to tag along and leave the organising to others, travelling with a friend who's an architecture buff, knowledgeable birdwatcher or talented gourmand can give you a wonderful appreciation for a place that you wouldn't have gained on your own.

Linking up with people on the road is the best of both worlds. A tried and tested formula for novice travellers is to take a tour, which enables you to meet people and acclimatise to the new surroundings, before venturing farther afield on your own.

Many a relationship has begun on the road, but the couple that travels together doesn't necessarily stay together. The reverse is also true. If you link up with someone *en route*, be as upfront as possible about your intentions. This will avoid heartbreak at the inevitable fork in the road. Also, don't take a trip with your partner to 'test' the relationship; that's putting it under too much strain. Spending 24/7 together, especially on a tough trip where even doing laundry is a logistical feat, will probably not do wonders for your relationship. And it's hard to enjoy travel when it's a romantic litmus test and your primary focus is your partner's happiness, rather than taking in the exotic surroundings.

Travel involves dozens of decisions every day: window or aisle seat; dorm room or double room; bus or train; where to go and what to see; how much to spend; when, where and what to eat. Each one is a potential disagreement for a couple – or any two people travelling together. Lolling around on a beach for five days is not everyone's idea of a fun trip, but that doesn't mean there's no hope for the relationship!

Know your partner's travel likes and dislikes

and, as much as possible, respect and accept each other's differences. If your partner is insufferable on long plane trips, the solution is simple: sit apart!

Deciding on a destination

This is the best bit. Destinations are often decided by the heart. But your passion for a place could be severely undermined unless you consider the factors of safety, season, time, budget and local culture.

Safety

The spectre of terrorism has elevated safety in the travel plans of people the world over. The devastation of the World Trade Centre attacks on 11 September 2001 and the Bali bombings of 12 October 2002 saw tragedy strike in places traditionally considered safe for travellers.

In this uncertain climate, government travel advisories assume even greater importance and are more vigilant about delivering information to travellers. Get the official word from your government about where travel is impossible or inadvisable. See the section titled 'Where to?' on page 10 for some useful online resources to help you make an informed decision.

All government travel advisories err on the side of caution and overstate the dangers, but have to be obeyed for insurance purposes. War groupies and adrenaline junkies should think long and hard about whether the thrill outweighs the worst-case scenario in a strife-torn land where your country has no official representation, and travel insurance isn't covering you because you've disregarded official warnings from your government to stay away.

The US State Department travel advisory is the most cautious (which was the case even before the terrorist attacks on New York and Washington), advising its citizens against travelling to twenty-five countries. Australia's Department of Foreign Affairs and Trade had travel warnings for seventeen countries as at November 2002, with heightened warnings for South-East Asian destinations, including all of Indonesia and parts of East Timor, Cambodia, Thailand, Malaysia and the Philippines, in the wake of the Bali bombings.

Farther afield, the 'war on terrorism', which began in October 2001, has made much of central

Asia a no-go zone. This extends to the disputed regions of Jammu and Kashmir, as well as the bordering Karakoram and Hindu Kush mountain ranges. Iraq and Pakistan are also best avoided. African nations where travel is either unsafe or impossible include Algeria, Angola, Burundi, Central African Republic, Ivory Coast, Liberia, Madagascar, Sierra Leone, Somalia and Sudan.

Hot spots and dangers exist in several other countries, including Albania, Bosnia, Yugoslavia, Bolivia, Colombia, Peru, Nepal, Sri Lanka and the Solomon Islands. If you are venturing to these parts, stay out of known danger zones. If you're unsure of which areas are dangerous, consider hiring a local driver or guide. If the locals won't venture to certain parts, neither should you.

Season
Study the climate and weather pattern of your intended destination. Sun and sea holidays are not a year-round option. The Greek islands are deserted over winter, and you might think twice about that cut-price tropical island getaway if it's in the middle of the monsoon season. Hiking in Nepal

is fairly limited to the dry months of April–May and October–November. Trekking in Patagonia is an activity for the southern summer, from December to February. East Africa's wildlife is best appreciated from June to September, between wet seasons.

Countries that cover a lot of latitude – the US, Mexico, China, India, Vietnam, Thailand, South Africa, Argentina and Chile, for example – have such variable conditions that you'll find pleasant spots year-round. As a general rule, for places with four seasons, spring and autumn are the best times to visit.

Find out whether you're travelling in the high, low or shoulder season. Wherever possible, avoid Europe in the July–August crush, unless you want to spend most of your time waiting in queues, paying exorbitant prices and begging for hotel rooms. Many restaurants, shops and other businesses in Europe close in August, when the world and his wife seem to descend on the Mediterranean. Don't even *think* about getting on a ferry to the Greek islands in August. North American beaches and national parks are also congested in July–August.

Remember to check whether your trip coincides

with school holidays or major festivals – such as Oktoberfest in Munich, Carnaval in Rio de Janeiro or Mardi Gras in New Orleans. You'll need to book accommodation well in advance – and pay rip-off rates.

Time

If your holiday runs to days rather than weeks, don't cram in too many far-flung destinations – this may seem obvious, but travellers do strange things when they get a whiff of jet fumes. Limit the air travel, time zones and climate changes. Doing Hawaii and Alaska in the same fortnight is asking for trouble. Apart from lugging gear for both the Arctic and the tropics, you'll spend your trip battling interminable jet lag.

Budget

Your destination could well be determined by the almighty dollar. Consider where you'll get the most travel mileage for your money. For Australians and New Zealanders, the exchange rate makes travel to Europe and the US extremely pricey, compared with Asia, Africa and island destinations in the Pacific and Indian oceans. After doing the sums, you may weigh up a week in the US against a month in India.

Local culture
Wherever you go, do some pre-departure research on your destination. Know something about its natural environment, laws, language, religion and customs. When you're in another country, its laws apply to you. You might want to note the location of the nearest home embassy.

Where to?
Some online resources for deciding on a destination:
www.dfat.gov.au
Australian Department of Foreign Affairs and Trade. For travel warnings, updates and all sorts of useful hints for Aussies abroad.
www.fco.gov.uk
British Foreign and Commonwealth Office. Comprehensive 'Traveller Tips' covering most countries and a section useful for Brits and non-Brits alike: 'When it All Goes Wrong'.

GETTING GOING 11

www.travel.state.gov
US State Department. An understandably more cautious view of the world. Detailed information on troubled regions.

www.mft.govt.nz
New Zealand Ministry of Foreign Affairs and Trade. Includes an index of NZ diplomatic posts worldwide and working holiday agreements with fifteen countries.

www.dfait-maeci.gc.ca
Canadian Department of Foreign Affairs and International Trade. Links to Canadian tourism and lists of Canadian diplomatic posts that can be useful to Aussies in places without Australian representation.

www.towd.com
Tourism Offices Worldwide Directory. Over 1440 up-to-date listings of national tourist offices, embassies, chambers of commerce and other sources of 'official' (i.e. not commercial) travel information.

www.itisnet.com
Internet Travellers Information Service. Aimed at backpackers and budget travellers. With country listings (some in need of updates), international airfares, general topics such as health and local customs and a travellers' network with bulletin board, news from the road, etc.

www.odci.gov/publications/factbook/index.html
CIA World Factbook. Amazing facts and figures on all countries, as well as incisive summaries, especially regarding trouble spots.

www.travel.world.co.uk
Impressive index of UK and Europe-based travel agents and tour operators. Contacts for all types of active and 'special experience' holidays – from safaris and study tours to birdwatching and battlefield tours. Hundreds of links to travel web sites, including accommodation listings, tourist offices and transport bookings.

www.visiteurope.com
Site of the European Travel Commission. Helpful sections on transport, planning your trip, the euro, specials etc., plus most countries' fast facts and figures, highlights and special events.

www.amerispan.com
AmeriSpan Unlimited is an 'educational travel company' specialising in Spanish-language travel programs and other cultural bridges. Partners include STA Australia, NZ and UK.

www.trailfinder.com
UK's largest independent travel company – also has

offices in Australia and Ireland. The site contains airfare specials to all continents, and more.

www.specialtytravel.com

For adventure and special-interest travellers, this site links countless destinations and a bewildering array of activities with over 500 tour operators around the globe. Also contains interesting articles from *Specialty Travel* magazine.

Planning an itinerary

Travel itineraries are like diets: great on paper but not always sensible and realistic. People tend to be overly ambitious, especially in Europe where the attractions, borders and cultures are so tightly packed together. The aim is not to see it all, but to appreciate all you see.

Flexibility in your schedule is essential and a sanity-saver. If you are flying somewhere and then joining a tour, give yourself a whole day at the destination to acclimatise and allow for flight delays and the like. Never plan it so you have to be in Mombasa on Monday at 6 p.m. to catch the last ferry to Zanzibar. Flexibility is also all-important for outdoor sights and activities. Don't set aside one day, and one day only, to climb Mount Olympus. When planning activities, consider the season. If you're trekking in the tropics in 90 per cent humidity, you should be planning two- or three-hour hikes rather than all-day affairs, especially early in the trip.

Try not to arrive at a new destination at night, particularly if you are female, travelling alone and don't speak the language. Consider pre-booking accommodation on the first night, especially after a long flight. You might fork out a bit more but you'll have rest and peace of mind. Avoid a rough start to your trip.

Adding some rest days is sensible for warding off 'If-it's-Tuesday-this-must-be-Belgium' syndrome. If you're in a city for three days, spend one day chilling out. It's amazing how much local flavour you can take in from a table at a café, or at a bustling market.

Avoid making urgent plans on days of travel, both before and after the journey. Allow plenty of time for transport delays, especially in developing countries.

If your time in some places is very limited, check that your must-see attraction is open the day you plan to visit. It's remarkable how many excited travellers turn up at the Louvre on Tuesdays, only to find it closed.

Gathering local contacts

Nothing beats touring around with a local: having that sense of slipping under the tourist radar and appreciating sights and scenes like an insider.

Before your trip, assemble a list of contacts in the countries you're visiting. Include relatives, friends, professional acquaintances and associations, and other potentially useful bodies, such as gay and lesbian organisations, women's traveller networks, or information and support groups for travellers with disabilities.

Add to your travel address book the nearest embassy of your home country, as well as accommodation options, especially recommendations from other travellers. This list will help you meet people and ease into your new surroundings. Call or write in advance of your visit.

chapter 2: TICKET TO RIDE

Getting the best fare

Buying your ticket direct from an airline is rarely the best deal. Airlines off-load fares they are not confident of selling at full price to travel agencies and specialists – and this is where you should start your search.

In Australia and New Zealand, Flight Centre and STA Travel are major players in cheap airfares. The UK has no shortage of travel discounters: Trailfinders, STA Travel and Council Travel are among the big ones.

Seek out agencies that specialise in your destination – Greece, South America, Vietnam, etc. – as they service the VFR (visiting friends and relatives) market and have the best deals. For off-the-beaten-track destinations and active holidays, try specialists such as Adventure World, Intrepid Travel or Peregrine Adventures. Check their excellent web sites, and get reports and recommendations from travellers. For other specialist tours (art and architecture, bird-watching, Jewish history, and so on), scan the travel sections of metropolitan newspapers.

The Internet has been a boon for travellers, allowing us to play travel agent at home. Often all you need do is fill in your destination, departure and arrival dates and your ticket is a keystroke away. For domestic travel, online bookings often represent the cheapest deals – the airlines basically cut out the travel agent and their commission.

International travel, however, is very different. Here the travel web sites function basically as online booking services; tickets are usually no cheaper than at travel agencies. Special deals do turn up, but these are typically short-term or last-minute, with many restrictions. The biggest general travel site is **www.travelocity.com**. Also check the web sites of the various airlines. Note that many air-travel sites cannot sell fares to residents of Australia and New Zealand.

However great that online deal may appear, it definitely pays to shop around and compare with agency prices. Ask about a round-the-world (RTW) fare, which is often great value, sometimes even cheaper than a return ticket. Most RTW tickets are valid for up to a year.

Advance-purchase tickets are cheapest (up to 40 per cent less than a full economy fare), although they carry certain restrictions. You might have to travel for more than fourteen days but no more than ninety or 180 days. You'll need to purchase the ticket about a month before your trip, and no stopovers are allowed. If you find a cheap ticket at the last minute, beware of the conditions attached. You could be flying to Heathrow via a fourteen-hour stopover in Harare.

Airlines online

Even if you don't buy your ticket direct from an airline, these web sites are a good starting point in your search for the best fare.

Aer Lingus **www.aerlingus.ie**
Aerolineas Argentinas **www.aerolineas.com.ar**

TICKET TO RIDE **19**

AeroMexico **www.aeromexico.com**
Air Canada **www.aircanada.ca**
Air France **www.airfrance.fr**
Air New Zealand **www.airnewzealand.co.nz**
Alitalia **www.alitalia.com**
American Airlines **www.aa.com**
Austrian Airlines Group **www.aua.com**
British Airways **www.britishairways.com**
Cathay Pacific **www.cathaypacific.com**
Continental Airlines **www.continental.com**
Delta Airlines **www.delta.com**
Finnair **www.finnair.fi**
Grupo Taca **www.grupotaca.com**
Iberia **www.iberia.com**
Icelandair **www.icelandair.net**
Japan Airlines **www.jal.com**
KLM **www.klm.com**
LanChile **www.lanchile.cl**
Lufthansa **www.lufthansa.com**
Malev Hungarian Airlines **www.malev.hu**
Mexicana Airlines **www.mexicana.com**
Northwest Airlines **www.nwa.com**
Olympic Airways **www.olympic-airways.gr**
QANTAS **www.qantas.com**

SN Brussels Airlines **www.dat-airlines.com**
SAS **www.scandinavian.net**
Singapore Airlines **www.singaporeair.com**
THY Turkish Airlines **www.turkishairlines.com**
United Airlines **www.ual.com**
Varig **www.varig.com**
Virgin Atlantic Airways **www.virgin-atlantic.com**

Countries with cheap fares

The UK is the home of bargain-basement airfares to Europe. Travel shops specialising in discounted fares are thick on the ground in London, and some great deals can be snapped up. If you intend travelling to the UK and on to Europe, you should consider buying your ticket in London. You can find these deals in traveller-oriented publications such as *TimeOut* and *TNT*, as well as the travel sections of newspapers. Hong Kong and Amsterdam are also home to many 'bucket shops' offering discounted air tickets.

Apart from these centres, cheap fares depend on the season, not the destination. Some countries may embark on marketing campaigns to entice visitors with cheap holidays (after a natural disaster or political coup, for example), but travel is largely seasonal. Check the Internet and newspaper ads for specials and cultivate a relationship with a travel agent, who can keep a lookout for good deals.

Travel patterns and prices to Europe are fairly fixed. The high season is from 1 June to 19 August, coinciding with the northern summer, and again from 7 December to mid-January. Top prices are determined by peak demand during summer, school and Christmas holidays. The low season is from mid-January to the end of February. Three shoulder seasons round out the calendar. Because these dates are quite fixed, the price of a ticket can drop dramatically depending on your departure date. For example, you can save up to $500 on your airfare by leaving on 31 May rather than 1 June.

Travel patterns to Asia and North America are very different. Short-term travel predominates in this market, so you can get cheap flights to Los Angeles, for example, almost any month of the year.

Look for good deals during the wet season. Fares and hotel rates in countries such as Vietnam and Thailand can drop dramatically even though some parts of the country remain dry and sunny.

Taking out travel insurance

Don't even *think* of leaving home without travel insurance. Having no insurance means you run the risk of paying for a holiday you don't end up taking, or losing your luggage, camera and other gear for good. Travel insurance provides peace of mind for these and other scenarios.

Travellers too often treat insurance as an afterthought, usually taking it out the day before departure. Never leave it to the last minute – it could be too late to cover you in the case of an industrial dispute, for example. Far more research should go into finding the best insurance policy, arguably more time than you spend on your ticket.

Cancellation cover is a must for those who've prepaid some or all of their holiday. All kinds of unexpected scenarios can befall you in the days before your departure and force you to cancel a non-refundable holiday package, like breaking a leg in a car accident, being struck by lightning on the golf course, or having a close friend or relative fall ill. An insurance bill of $200 could save you $1000 in cancellation penalties.

Make sure the policy also includes lost-luggage and theft cover. If you are taking an expensive camera or computer with you, cover for the value of the goods. Photographers, birdwatchers and other travellers with valuable equipment should consider taking out specialist cover. If you intend to buy cameras, computers and other gadgets on your travels, make sure the policy will cover the new gear also. Send home a copy of the receipts and serial numbers as proof of ownership.

When purchasing insurance, always question what's free, or what comes 'included'. Many travellers who buy airfares with their credit card assume they are covered because the ticket comes with travel insurance, courtesy of the credit provider – but what exactly is the cover? There could well be a $500 excess on each claim; in other words, not much cover at all. Similarly, some personal and home insurance policies claim to provide travel cover as well. Check what exactly you are covered for – or more importantly, *not* covered for.

A true travel policy, with no excess charges, provides the best cover. Full insurance, however, is becoming increasingly expensive. After weighing your options, you might decide to go with a cheaper policy and bear the excess charges. If all goes well, you'll save some money.

Of course, cutting insurance costs means a decision on where to cut cover. Never compromise on full medical cover. Consider instead reduced cover for theft and/or lost luggage.

Lastly, always read the fine print, or get a travel agent to decipher it for you. Some insurance companies will refuse to cover you if you disregard official travel warnings, or undertake 'high risk' or 'dangerous' activities (see chapter 4 for more on specific health insurance). Carefully check the claim requirements of the policy. You may need a police report to claim for theft, receipts for medical bills and so on.

chapter 3: TRAVEL DOCUMENTS AND MONEY

Passports

Apply for a passport or renew your existing one well ahead of your trip. Passports must be valid for at least six months from the time you enter another country – sometimes more.

Australians can apply for passports at post offices and at passport offices in major cities. Expect a wait of three weeks and a charge of around $120. Passports are valid for ten years. New Zealanders can obtain a passport application from travel agents. The cost is around NZ$80. Britons apply at post offices and pay around £30.

You must produce a passport when entering

and leaving a country. You'll also need it for checking into accommodation and cashing traveller's cheques, so look after it. Keep it inside a plastic cover to avoid moisture, especially if you're carrying it in a cotton or leather money belt. In this time of anti-terrorist vigilance, more countries are refusing entry if the passport appears worn, untidy or tampered with. Never alter your passport, or hand it over as security for a debt.

To avoid losing all ID at once, keep your passport separate from traveller's cheques and credit cards. Keep one photocopy in your luggage and another with friends or relatives back home. Take a spare pile of passport photos with you – these can be incredibly useful when applying abroad for visas, among other things.

If your passport is lost or stolen, report it to local police and take the police report to the nearest Australian diplomatic post.

Visas

A visa is a stamp or document affixed to a passport granting official permission for foreigners to enter and travel in (or transit) a country for a specified time. Visa regulations are complex and ever-changing. Always check the latest requirements with a travel agent or an embassy of the country you wish to visit.

Many visas have been phased out in the last few years, especially for short-stay travel between Western nations. Travellers can stay up to six months in some countries without a visa. In contrast, some countries require a visa even for transit stops. The following is a general guide.

Africa

Most countries require visas of Australians and New Zealanders. The exceptions are Botswana, Gambia, Malawi, Morocco, Namibia, South Africa, Swaziland, Tunisia, Uganda, Zambia and Zimbabwe. Egypt issues visas on arrival. In addition to a visa, to enter most countries in Africa you will need to show proof of vaccination against yellow fever and/or cholera. Some countries may also want to see an onward ticket or itinerary, and in rare cases, a letter of invitation. Some visas need to be obtained before you arrive in Africa so check out the requirements well in advance.

Asia

No two Asian countries have the same visa regulations. Virtually everyone needs a visa to enter Bhutan, China, India, Myanmar, Nepal, Pakistan and Vietnam. Bhutan allows a maximum stay of just fifteen days, compared with India's six months. Vietnam visas are for thirty days, and your visit must fall between the specified arrival and departure dates.

Other countries – Bangladesh, Brunei, Cambodia, Laos, Mongolia – issue visas on arrival. Find out how long this entitles you to stay – the Laotian visa is for fifteen days, and an extension must be arranged before you leave home.

Visa-free travel in South Korea and Taiwan is only for fourteen days; in the Philippines it is twenty-one days. The least restrictive countries for Australians and New Zealanders are Japan and Sri Lanka (ninety days visa-free), Malaysia and Indonesia (up to sixty days), Singapore (thirty days) and Thailand (thirty to ninety days).

Europe

EU countries allow thirty to ninety days' travel

without a visa, but always carry your passport. Some countries in eastern Europe – namely the Czech Republic, Hungary, Latvia, Macedonia, Poland, Romania and Slovakia – still require visas of Australians and New Zealanders. In some cases, visas are issued at point of entry. Find out before you go.

Central and South America
Only Brazil, Nicaragua, Paraguay, Suriname and Uruguay require visas of Australians and New Zealanders; Britons travel visa-free. But it still pays to check specifics: Venezuela, for instance, allows most Westerners arriving by air to enter visa-free, while those travelling overland must have visas.

North America
Australians and citizens of many other Western countries can travel visa-free to the US for up to ninety days and Canada for up to six months.

Visas are usually issued at an embassy of the country you wish to visit, while you wait. Nonetheless, Australians and New Zealanders should try to obtain most visas before leaving home. It's a risk to buy expensive rail or air tickets without first obtaining a visa. And it means you won't waste travel days waiting in queues at the visa section of an embassy with bafflingly irregular hours. However, some embassies will want to see a return ticket or proof of sufficient funds to last your stay before issuing a visa.

Be sure to obtain the correct visa for your intended stay. Some questions to ask when applying for a visa are: Does the visa take effect from the date of issue or from the date of entry? Do you require a single-entry or multiple-entry visa? As a visa-bearer, will you need to register with the local police once you are in the country? What is the charge, if any?

Remember, even if you have the all-important stamp or document, a visa is not a guarantee of entry. Your behaviour at the point of entry may arouse suspicion; your dress may not comply to local standards, or your passport could contain a visa from an unfriendly neighbour. Several countries – Malaysia, Tunisia and Libya among them – refuse to grant entry to citizens of Israel; even an Israeli visa in your passport can result in barred entry. Some countries deny entry to travellers who are HIV positive.

Travelling visa-free does not mean footloose and fancy free. Visa or not, your stay comes with conditions attached regarding the purpose and duration of your visit. Carrying your CV on a visa-free 'holiday', for instance, will arouse suspicion and possibly see you turned back at the border.

It's in your interest to be honest when applying for a visa and to adhere to its conditions. Your own government cannot intervene in situations where visas have been denied or visits terminated. That is totally the province of each country's immigration officials. Deportation is at the expense of the deported.

Working overseas

Well before your trip, contact an embassy of the country where you wish to work. Volunteer, aid and cultural-exchange organisations can also be helpful.

Australia has reciprocal working-holiday agreements with Canada, Ireland, Japan, Malta, the Netherlands, South Korea and the UK. These allow Australians to work during part of a holiday.

Arrangements vary from country to country, but in most cases you are allowed to work only for part of your stay, and not in your trade or profession (which requires a working visa). These agreements are intended to help fund your trip, rather than further your career. Check with the relevant embassy or high commission before you set off. New Zealand has working-holiday arrangements with fifteen countries.

Britain has allowed hordes of young Aussies and Kiwis, with at least one British-born grandparent, to work in Britain without a work permit, though they must apply for entry. Similarly, all Commonwealth citizens aged between seventeen and twenty-seven can apply to be 'working holiday-makers' and stay in Britain for up to two years, but are only permitted to work for half that time.

Like Britain, certain EU countries grant privileges (work permits or citizenship) to children or grandchildren of their nationals. If you are of German, Greek or Irish descent, contact the relevant embassy and ask about your status.

Whether you're thinking of aid work in Africa

or being an *au pair* in Austria, get your hands on a specialist title that deals with working abroad (see 'Working titles' below).

Vacation Work Publications (**www.vacationwork.co.uk**) boasts around sixty titles, most of them about working, studying and living overseas. Their 'Live & Work Abroad' series has eleven titles and there are annual guides to summer jobs in Britain, the US and abroad. Also try the Australian-based Global Exchange (**www.globalexchange.com.au**).

Working titles

Check a travel bookshop, library or publishers' web site for these guides to working abroad.

The Au Pair & Nanny's Guide to Working Abroad, by S. Griffith & S. Legg (Vacation Work Publications, 1997).
Getting a Job Abroad, by R. Jones (How To Books, 1996).
Getting a Job in Europe, by M. Hempshett (How To Books, 2000).
Japan: A Working Holiday Guide, by L. Southerden (Global Exchange, 2001).

34 TRAVEL TIPS

Live & Work Abroad – A Guide for Modern Nomads,
by H. Francis and M. Callan
(Vacation Work Publications, 2001).

Live & Work in Saudi and the Gulf, by L. Whetter
(Vacation Work Publications, 2000). Other titles in this
series: *Australia & New Zealand*; *Belgium, the
Netherlands & Luxembourg*; *France*; *Germany*; *Italy*;
Japan; *Russia & Eastern Europe*; *Scandinavia*; *Scotland*;
Spain & Portugal; *USA & Canada*.

Living & Working in Britain, by C. Hall
(How To Books, 2002).

Living & Working in Germany, by C. Hall
(How To Books, 2001).

Taking a Gap Year, by S. Griffith
(Vacation Work Publications, 2000).

Teaching English Abroad, by S. Griffith
(Vacation Work Publications, 1996).

Volunteer Work Overseas, by P. Hodge et al
(Global Exchange, 1998).

Workaway Guide by K. Halliday. A guide for Australians.

Working & Eating in Tuscany & Umbria,
by J. Lasdun and P. Davis (Penguin, 1997).

Work Your Way Around the World, by S. Griffith
(Vacation Work Publications, 2001).

Traveller's cheques versus cards

Many travellers don't use traveller's cheques anymore. The proliferation of ATMs and international networks means travellers can conveniently withdraw money in the local currency as they go along.

But traveller's cheques haven't yet outlived their usefulness. They offer protection against theft. They can be used outside banking hours and in places where banks are few and far between. They are more readily accepted in destinations (like Africa) where cards can be of limited use. And in many cases the exchange rate can be better for cheques than for cash.

The longer your trip, and the farther off the beaten track you go, the more likely you'll need some traveller's cheques. If you're abroad for several months, it's unlikely you can survive on just a debit or credit card.

It's best to have a combination of traveller's cheques, cash and cards. Take both a credit card and a debit card linked to the Cirrus or Plus system so you can access cash abroad. Ask your bank whether you can get cash advances abroad on your credit card (and what it will cost in fees or interest rates). Finally, keep your cards, cash and cheques separate in case of theft.

Negotiating fluctuating exchange rates

The January 2002 introduction of the euro meant the demise of twelve European currencies, among them the world's oldest currency, the 2600-year-old drachma. But the euro is a godsend for travellers. Instead of spending half your European holiday queuing at banks and exchange bureaux swapping deutschmarks for drachmas, Irish pounds for pesetas, lira for markka and schillings for guilder, the euro is the only currency you'll need throughout much of Western and central Europe.

The official currency of 300 million people in twelve nations – Belgium, Germany, Greece, Spain, France, Ireland, Italy, Austria, Portugal, Luxembourg, the Netherlands and Finland – the euro makes it easier to compare prices across borders, and it saves travellers a heap in exchange rates and commissions.

In the rest of Europe and in Asia, Africa and

South America, you can go nuts dealing with the mathematical gymnastics of fluctuating exchange rates. The only constant in this equation is the law of diminishing returns. When changing money, you can lose a chunk of change in various ways: flat fees, a percentage of the transaction, minimum fees and the exchange rate itself. Some places charge no transaction fee but offer a lousy exchange rate. Others have hefty charges but competitive rates. Depending on the sum you're changing, you'll need to calculate which is the best deal for you. Some general tips are:

- Limit your losses in commissions and exchange rates by reducing your transactions. Pay for big purchases (accommodation, travel tickets, hire car) with your credit card.
- Big banks (the bigger the better) generally offer the best rate of exchange. Avoid changing money at hotels. Airports too are often more expensive than banks. The convenience factor at airports is sometimes decisive, but if you can, wait until you get into town to change money.
- Money-changing facilities rarely include their fees in advertised rates. The only question you

need to ask is: 'If I give you X amount in this currency, what will I end up with?'
- For traveller's cheques, find out whether a fee is slugged per cheque or per transaction. Avoid the former, especially for small bills. Change bigger notes where possible and practical. Bigger bills sometimes mean a better exchange rate.
- Find out how much currency rates can fluctuate in certain countries. If there is little variation (as in Thailand, for example), don't waste your time running between banks, exchange centres and street moneychangers. Check the money section of the local paper to find out where you can get the best rates.
- Coins might as well be Monopoly money once you cross a border. Banks do not exchange foreign coinage. Change or spend them before you leave the country.

Euro exchange rates (as at November 2002)
1 euro = 1.79AUD; 2.01NZD; 1.00USD; 0.64GBP; 1.59CAD; 122JPY.

The euro

The arrival of the euro on 1 January 2002 saw the greatest currency exchange in history, with twelve national currencies in Europe replaced by just one. The national notes and coins were swiftly replaced by 14.5 billion rainbow-coloured euro banknotes and 56 billion euro coins. The banknotes come in seven denominations ranging from five to 500 euros. There are eight coins, ranging from two euros to one cent. While the banknotes are identical across all twelve countries, coins retain national symbols on one face.

Considering the scale of the task – converting to euros the financial accounts of 300 million people, and re-programming ATMs, vending machines, parking meters and cash registers – the transition was remarkably smooth. Ironically, many Europeans found themselves with outdated wallets, rather than cash. The euro notes, wider than some of the old national bills, did not fit in old wallets. In Italy, this led to great sales of leather wallets and some ironical musings: decades ago, it was the old lira notes (so large they were dubbed 'handkerchiefs' and 'sheets') that had to be folded into quarters to fit into most wallets.

Online currency converter

For online foreign-exchange calculations, go to the Universal Currency Converter: **www.xe.net/ucc**. Rates are updated every minute.

Having a back-up

Some hardened travellers have been known to carry an ID 'decoy' – complete with expired passport, a wallet containing cancelled or expired credit cards and some small bills. This is then handed over to thieves or kept in a back pocket or empty camera case for them to help themselves. While you probably don't need to go to these lengths, you do need to think about minimising the damage if your travel documents and money are lost or stolen.

First rule: keep your money and travel documents apart. Also separate your cash, traveller's cheques and cards. You should carry your passport at all times. But there's no need to take piles of traveller's cheques and all your cards with you if you're just going out for a walk, especially if your hotel has a safe. Take only what you need; that way you won't lose everything.

Make two photocopies of your passport and

bank cards: keep one in your luggage and leave the other with friends or relatives at home. If you have traveller's cheques, also leave a list of serial numbers with someone at home, and be sure to update the list on the road, crossing off the cheques as you cash them.

The advantage with traveller's cheques is that they are far easier to replace than lost bank cards. Keep an emergency stash of $200 or so in your luggage. If two or more of you are travelling, consider reserving one bank card for emergency use only. Alternatively, before you leave home, ask your bank if you can have two cards to access your account. Keep the emergency card in your luggage or leave it at home for friends to send to you.

Wills and power of attorney

More and more travellers, regardless of age, are making or updating their will before going abroad, especially since the terrorist attacks of 11 September 2001.

When you think about it, the reasons for making a will in the first place are even more valid for travellers. On top of the grief, you don't want to leave your loved ones with financial and organisational burdens in case of death overseas. In Australia, if you die intestate, a strict formula determines where your assets go. See a lawyer or ask at government bookshops in major cities for a do-it-yourself will kit. Some newsagents also have them.

Power of attorney comes in three types: general, enduring, and enduring specifically for medical procedures. For long-term travellers, general power of attorney is a good idea. This means appointing someone to act on your behalf, for finalising property transfers, for example, or signing tax returns and jury forms. Again, see a lawyer or ask where to get a power-of-attorney kit.

chapter 4: HEALTH

Insurance

We'll say it again: if you don't have travel insurance, you shouldn't be travelling.

Travellers think small when it comes to health insurance – for example, a sprained ankle or food poisoning – instead of the worst-case scenario, such as contracting malaria, having a heart attack, or being struck by a car in the US and having to sell the house to pay the medical bills. Imagine an attack of acute appendicitis while trekking in Nepal – without insurance, a medical evacuation like this is a physical and financial ordeal.

Proper travel insurance will cover for unlimited medical costs, with no excess. Make sure the cover includes overseas medical and dental treatment, local hospitalisation and medical evacuation. Get cover for pre-existing conditions where possible.

Australia has reciprocal health agreements with New Zealand and seven European nations. This allows Australian citizens to access the public health system in these countries. But the trips to hospital and time in care don't come free! You *still* need travel insurance.

For adventure travel – hiking, cycling, rafting, canyoning or mountaineering – be upfront about the activities you will undertake and purchase the appropriate cover. Young travellers, despite being the biggest risk-takers, often go uninsured.

Check the fine print of the policy for activities which are considered 'risky' and require extra cover. For many policies, walking in high heels on cobblestones is considered just short of death-defying. Study the claim requirements of the policy. You may need to produce accident or medical reports, receipts for medical bills, and so on.

Vaccinations

To find out if you need pre-trip vaccinations, see your GP or visit your local travellers' medical and vaccination centre (online at **www.tmvc.com.au**). Also check the web site of the World Health Organisation at **www.who.org**.

Start your enquiries early, as some vaccinations can take several weeks or even months. Rabies and Hepatitis C, for example, require a course of three injections. If you're travelling to sub-Saharan Africa, the tropics in South America or certain parts of Asia, you'll need many jabs and they have to be spaced apart to minimise reaction and to give your pin-cushion arm time to recover. Antimalarial medication needs to be taken up to a month before you leave home. And remember, the jabs don't come cheap, especially for families.

Make sure all your vaccinations are recorded in an official certificate. Although vaccination for cholera is no longer recommended nor said to be required, several countries in Africa and South America deny entry without proof of vaccination against it.

Getting in shape before you go

You wouldn't book a golf holiday if you don't play golf. Similarly, if you've booked a trek in the

Himalayas, you should know the physical requirements and do the prep work, or you won't enjoy the trip.

As much as possible beforehand, simulate the activity you'll be doing while you're away. If that's hiking, your preparation should include bushwalking in hilly terrain, and climbing sandhills and stairs.

If you're trekking in tropical jungle, jogging and some weights work in a gym will help your endurance in the humidity. It's the regularity of the exercise that's important, not the duration or exertion.

If you're headed for Europe, buy a good pair of walking shoes (probably the best thing you can do for your health) and wear them in before you hit the cobblestones. Many travellers are hobbled after walking in new shoes for more kilometres in one day than they would in a week at home.

Finally, be sure to visit your dentist before you leave. Emergency dental work in the back of beyond is the stuff of nightmares – just think root canal without novocaine.

Travelling with medication

If you need to take medication, bring a prescription from your doctor and, if possible, a letter explaining why you need medication and how long you've been using it. This is important if you're headed for a country where your medication could be illegal.

Make sure your script has the drug's generic name, not just the brand name. Do some research or ask your doctor about whether the medication is readily available at your destination. If not, you'll need to take a plentiful supply.

Don't forget to also ask your doctor or travel agent about using over-the-counter drugs that may be illegal or prescription-only in other countries. Vicks inhalers, for instance, are banned in Japan as they contain a substance considered to be a stimulant. In some countries, headache tablets containing codeine are strictly prescription-only.

Packing a medical kit

Hikers, campers and others venturing off the beaten path should bring a well-equipped medical kit.

These are available at traveller health centres. You can buy a basic kit and add to it, or make one up yourself. Some suggested inclusions are as follows.

- Your regular medication, complete with prescriptions and possibly a letter from your doctor confirming your condition and treatment.
- Aspirin for headaches, pain and fever.
- Antimalarials and possibly a malaria diagnosis kit.
- Antidiarrhoea medications (also known as 'stoppers' or 'blockers'). The most common brands are Imodium and Lomotil.
- Antiseptic cream or lotion for cuts and scratches.
- Antibiotics for bacterial infections, especially ear, throat and chest. See your doctor about whether you should take antibiotics and which types are best. You'll need a prescription. Antibiotics have no effect on viral infections, which include most colds and some strains of gastric flu.
- Antihistamines for allergies such as hay fever, as well as preventing motion sickness and itching of insect bites.

HEALTH

- Rehydration mixture for bad cases of diarrhoea and dehydration in hot weather.
- Decongestant for colds.
- Sunscreen, lip balm and eye drops.
- Throat lozenges.
- Insect repellent.
- A compact book on travel health.

The best way to deal with sickness is to not get sick. Notice that most of the items in your medical kit are about prevention rather than cure or treatment. You should boost prevention by watching your everyday health. This can be summed up as follows.

- Get good rest – give yourself a chance to recover from abrupt changes in time, climate, culture and food. Think hard about a third straight night of sleeping on the train.
- Drink plenty of fluids, preferably bottled water, especially in hot climates.
- Wash your hands regularly (especially after visiting the toilet) and avoid contact with the face.
- Take multivitamins to compensate for dietary changes and deficiencies.
- Remember to take your regular medications.

Water and food

Delhi belly, the Orient Express, the Transylvania trots . . . traveller's diarrhoea has many names but only a couple of likely causes: contaminated food and water. Dysentery, cholera, typhoid and hepatitis A and E are some of the diarrhoeal diseases that can result from contaminated food. Sanitation, refrigeration and food-handling standards are lacking in many developing countries. Basically, the poorer the country the more care you need to take. But follow a few commonsense rules and you should stay pretty healthy.

First rule: be scrupulous about washing your hands after visiting the bathroom and before eating. Even outside meal times, keep your hands away from your face.

You should have some idea before you arrive at your destination as to whether tap water is safe to drink. If unsure, assume it's not safe. Ice is also unsafe, as freezing doesn't destroy germs. Don't put ice in drinks or even use it to chill food. Don't brush your teeth with dodgy tap water. Stick to bottled water if possible. Go for brands you recognise over the local product, which may be only marginally better than tap water. Check the seal – make sure you don't have a refilled bottle. If bottled water isn't an option, you'll have to boil the tap water. Keep it at a rolling boil for several minutes. Don't just bring it to the boil – it *is* possible to get sick from cups of tea or coffee. Many accommodation houses in Asia and Africa will provide boiled water. Those veering way off the beaten track on hiking and camping trips should purify water with chlorine or iodine tablets.

Food is trickier. If you're going away for weeks or months, constantly buying meals prepared by others, chances are you'll get sick from a dodgy meal, rather than water. Price is not always a reliable indicator of good hygiene standards. A hotel buffet, where the food could be left at room temperature for hours, is a greater risk than freshly cooked food from a street vendor.

The most important rule is to buy food that's freshly prepared and piping hot, whether it comes from a roadside stall or a four-star hotel. Danger foods are undercooked red meat, raw fish and shellfish. Salmonella thrives in lukewarm chicken, pork, cream and rice. Avoid anything that's been left at room temperature or reheated, such as sandwiches with meat.

Raw vegetables are risky because they're difficult to clean, or they could be washed with contaminated water. Cooked vegies, though, are fairly safe. Avoid all salads. Stick to fruit you can peel. Be aware that local milk could be unpasteurised. Powdered or long-life milk is a safe alternative.

Be cautious but not afraid to eat the local food. It's amazing how the most paranoid travellers can still get sick, and how often travellers come a cropper after lashing out on a 'Western' meal such as hamburgers. Food is an essential, enriching part of the travel experience. A case of diarrhoea is all too common on the road and could be the result of several factors – such as big changes in climate, time zone and diet – and not necessarily bad food.

Recovering from common ailments

Although most travellers live in fear of contracting some obscure tropical disease, the most common traveller ailments are diarrhoea, colds and flu, heat exhaustion, insect bites and foot problems.

Diarrhoea
Diarrhoea on a trip is as inevitable as a customs queue. It can range from traveller's diarrhoea (caused by stress, jet lag or a big change in diet – in which case there's no cause for concern) to amoebic dysentery (bloody diarrhoea caused by a parasite in food and water, which attacks the liver or brain in the most severe cases). Symptoms of the more serious types of diarrhoea can take a week or longer to emerge, unlike traveller's diarrhoea or food poisoning, which come on rather suddenly.

Contaminated food and water are the most common causes of diarrhoea. Beware also of contaminated food utensils, which could be more suspect than the actual food. For this reason, many travellers bring their own bowl and cutlery.

The best treatment for diarrhoea is to rest, preferably within lunging distance of a loo, and drink plenty of fluids. If you're dashing to the toilet more than six times a day, take a rehydration mixture. When your appetite returns, stick to bland, starchy foods. Take note of other more serious symptoms – headaches, high fever, bloating, all-over aches and pains.

If you have to keep moving – on a hiking trip or a long bus journey – you'll have to resort to 'stoppers'. Treat antidiarrhoeals with caution – they are for short-term use only. Diarrhoea is the body's way of flushing out infection. Prolonged use of stoppers can cause side-effects and more serious complications.

Colds and flu

Although these terms are used interchangeably, they are different illnesses. Flu symptoms include a high temperature, headache and general aches and pains. You can feel sapped of energy long after the symptoms have cleared. A cold involves a sore throat, runny nose and cough. You can also have cold symptoms with the flu.

Both colds and flu are viral infections, which means antibiotics are useless in treating them, although you may need antibiotics for secondary infections of the ear or upper respiratory tract.

The best treatment is to rest and let the virus run its course. Drink plenty of fluids, especially teas with honey and/or lemon. Throat lozenges and nasal decongestants will ease symptoms.

Heat exhaustion
Going from winter to summer can put you at risk of sunburn and heat exhaustion. Drink plenty of fluids – it's a slippery slope from dehydration to heatstroke. Thirst is not an indicator of how much you need to drink. Wear loose, light clothing, a hat, sunglasses and plenty of sunscreen. If you're older or not in the best physical shape, consider taxis to shorten some trips. Don't walk everywhere in oppressive heat. Take a rehydration mixture if you're hit by heat exhaustion. If you start feeling worse – with severe headache, nausea, shivering, drowsiness – you may need to be rehydrated with an IV drip in hospital.

Insect bites
With mosquito-borne diseases (malaria, dengue fever), the focus is on prevention rather than cure. Avoid bites by covering up, wearing light-coloured

clothing, using mosquito nets and repellent and taking antimalarial medication. If you're trekking in jungle areas, you may need to have your clothes, mosquito nets and other equipment treated with insecticide. Be especially careful at dusk and night (although dengue mosquitoes bite during the day). It's important to avoid scratching the bite as it could lead to infection. If bites are accompanied by headaches, nausea or fever, get out your malaria diagnosis kit if you have one, or seek a doctor for the simple blood test that can diagnose malaria. Note that malarial symptoms can take a week or longer to present.

Foot problems
If your feet are killing you, they're probably killing your enjoyment of the trip as well. Walking on a cushion of blisters makes it hard to look at anything but your tortured feet.

Be careful in your choice of shoe. Unless you're hiking almost every day, don't bother with hard walking boots. Remember that feet and ankles swell considerably in heat. Also make sure your socks are absorbent – if you can, try wearing two pairs. Wash your feet daily and dry them carefully. Resist the urge to pierce or peel blisters – the skin is the best dressing.

For most traveller ailments, rest is the best remedy. Pay for a better room if you have to – for example, one with a private bathroom if you're suffering from diarrhoea. Some pharmacies can suggest over-the-counter treatments for minor ailments. If, despite your best efforts, your condition hasn't improved in about forty-eight hours, you should look at getting to a doctor. Larger hotels the world over have doctors on call, or you can ask at your embassy for English-speaking doctors.

chapter 5: TRAVEL GUIDES

What's on the market

Never before has so much of the world's population travelled the globe. And never before have so many travellers embarked on their journeys clutching guidebooks. These are halcyon days for travel guides. Whether it's honeymooners, backpackers, gap-year travellers, working holidaymakers, drivers, divers, cyclists, hikers, shoppers, gourmands, art and architecture buffs, kid travellers or pet travellers, there's a guidebook out there for them all.

Guidebooks can be very useful, however dependency on them these days can verge on the ridiculous. Somewhere along the way, 'guide' became 'gospel', with some travellers rarely taking their nose out of the book for long enough to actually experience, as opposed to just reading about, a place. Don't assume a sight or business isn't worthy just because it's not listed in a guide. In fact, if you were to stick to the guidebook trails, you'd see far more fellow travellers than locals. The best places are often those you discover yourself.

Nevertheless, guidebooks contain so much excellent information and insight that they can be indispensable – as anyone who's arrived at a dingy railway station in the dead of night can attest. It's only smart to take a look at what's out there when planning your trip.

When buying a guidebook, assess the split of destination versus practical information. The more lavishly illustrated the guide, the thinner the section on accommodation, restaurant listings and other useful visitor information. That's fine if your trip is only for a fortnight or so to one country, region or city. But if you're on the road for weeks or months, moving almost every other day and lining up your own accommodation, you should look for a guidebook with detailed listings. So too if you're headed for a remote destination with little tourism infrastructure, such as Mongolia.

Also, check the tone of the writing – how much opinion and recommendation is in there? Some guides give detailed coverage of the sights but no sense of whether it's worth going out of your way to see them, or how much time to allow while you're there.

Finally, check the publication date of the guide. Some titles are on three or even five-year cycles. If you can't decide between two guides, pick the newer one. And regardless of how recent the book is, always adjust the prices upwards.

As no bookshop has the shelf space to stock the voluminous title list of even one of the big publishers, you should check the web sites for the title you need. Some of the major players in guidebooks are as follows.

AA (www.theAA.com)

Published by Britain's Automobile Association, which claims to be 'Britain's largest travel publisher', the 300 or so AA guides come in many guises. The different series include B&B guides, Best Drives, Caravan & Camping, as well as Spiral

Guides, Travel Packs and City Packs. The latter are colour pocket guides covering top sights and highlights of popular destinations, with a large fold-out map included. The destinations are fairly mainstream, so there are plenty of alternatives.

Eyewitness (www.dk.com)

Produced by Dorling Kindersley (DK), these glossy, lavishly illustrated guides 'show you what others only tell you'. Most titles are packed with over 1000 photos and include floor plans of major sights. They are big on history, must-see sights, other highlights and walking tours, but a bit light on for practical information. They are also hefty – in both weight and price. Great for sightseeing and pre-trip or armchair reading.

Fodors (www.fodors.com)

Founded by Hungarian-born Eugene Fodor in 1936 and now published by Random House, Fodors claims to be the 'world's largest English-language travel information provider'. Its twelve series (not including maps and phrasebooks) include roughly 300 titles. Of these, more than

220 cover the US, Canada and Europe. The Gold Guides, numbering over a hundred titles, are the most widely sold. Updated every year and penned by local writers, they offer a mix of cultural and practical information, and reviews of accommodation and eating options in all price ranges. They also contain advertising, little colour and are thinner than other guidebooks.

Footprint (www.footprintbooks.com)

Based in Bath, UK, Footprint guides were formerly known as Travel & Trade Publications. Latin American specialists, their flagship *South American Handbook* was first published in 1920 and is the world's longest-running guidebook in English (once featuring updates from Graham Greene). The current 78th edition runs to more than 1600 tissue-thin pages and contains over 170 city and regional maps. Footprint aims for 'the ultimate practical guidebook'. The nineteen Latin American titles and nineteen Asian titles dominate the sixty-strong title list. A few city guides have recently rolled out but these face stiff competition from established titles.

Frommer's (www.frommers.com)

Arthur Frommer pioneered budget travel in 1957 with his *Europe on $5 a Day*. The latest edition (2002) is *Europe on $70 a Day*, a stark comment on how times, and guidebooks, move on. Frommer's is no longer the last word on budget travel and its no-frills design and presentation is a little hard to navigate. The title list numbers over 300 books split between no less than eighteen series. The style, layout and territory covered is similar to Fodors.

Insight (www.insightguides.com)

Renowned for wonderful photography, Insight Guides have been around since 1970 and are closest in feel and design to Eyewitness. Lovely to look at, as you'd expect of 'visual travel guides', they feature much historical and cultural information as well as gatefold colour maps. Like Eyewitness, only about 10 per cent of content is devoted to practical information such as accommodation and eating listings. The Classic series numbers over 200 titles, and apart from the usual suspects, includes out-of-the-way titles such as *Amazon Wildlife*, *Gambia & Senegal*, *Waterways of Europe* and *Marine Life of the South China Sea*.

Let's Go (www.letsgo.com)

Let's Go was established in 1960 when a group of Harvard students pooled their travel journals and tips to produce *Let's Go Europe*, a guide for other students on European vacations. *Let's Go Europe* has since been through forty-two editions and several translations and is by far the biggest-selling guidebook, especially popular with Americans and Canadians. A team of 300 students writes the books, which helps explain the budget-conscious selections and political opinions. Maps are not super-detailed and the title list, at around sixty, is not huge but the books are updated every year.

Lonely Planet (www.lonelyplanet.com)

Unlike the other major players, LP is based in Australia, with publishing offices also in London, Paris and Oakland. Established in 1972, LP initially specialised in Australasia, off-the-beaten track destinations and long-haul travel, but in recent years its title list has mushroomed into the most comprehensive and far-reaching of all. Whatever your destination, LP has the book. Its 'firsts' include guidebooks to Antarctica and Cuba, among others.

Does any other publisher devote whole titles to the Arctic, Botswana, Malawi or Mongolia? Apart from in-depth country, city and regional guides, LP produces condensed colour guides to major cities, guides for first-time travellers, walking and trekking guides, cycling guides, diving and snorkelling guides and multicountry guides, such as the *Africa*, *Europe*, *South-East Asia* and *South America* tomes. Strengths include knowledgeable, irreverent writing, user-friendly format and very generous outlay of detailed maps.

Michelin (www.viamichelin.co.uk)

This famous French company first produced *Le Guide Rouge* in 1900. Today there are twelve Red Guides rating hotels and restaurants, including a multicountry title covering twenty European nations and sixty-seven towns. The Green Guides are the car-touring companion to the Red Guides. Packed with maps and pics of splendid sights and scenery, they are rather pricey and scant with accommodation and eating options, which are listed for just the major towns. Green Guides cover every corner of France (fourteen regional titles),

Europe (twenty-nine titles) and North America (fourteen titles). In addition, Michelin produces thirty-eight In Your Pocket Guides for 'short-break destinations'. These are colourful and compact but the priciest pocket guide by far. The Neos series (ten titles) is attractively presented and aimed at a younger, adventurous crowd headed for more exotic destinations – titles include *Cuba; Guatemala & Belize; Rajasthan; Sri Lanka & the Maldives; Syria & Jordan*, among others.

Moon (www.moon.com)

California-based Moon guides are similar to Lonely Planet in content, feel, and even design, though the title list (around a hundred) does not approach LP's. With comprehensive coverage of history, arts, people, land and social issues, as well as detailed practical listings, they are for long-term travellers and those who want a big dose of local culture. Definitely consider Moon if you're headed to Mexico – there are no fewer than ten regional guides. The US is also well covered, with close to fifty guides, including such specific titles as *Big Island of Hawaii, Tahoe, Silicon Valley, Columbia River Gorge* and the *Grand Canyon*.

Rough Guides (www.roughguides.com)

London-based and part of the Penguin group, Rough Guides are renowned for their superb coverage of Europe, though there are more than a few Asian, African, Australian and North American titles in among the 150-plus travel guides. Strengths include lively writing, clean graphics and a youthful outlook. Rough Guides led the way with guides to Europe and Asia for first-time travellers, as well as a guide for female travellers. The stable also boasts a gay guide – *Gay & Lesbian Australia*. You'll find a good split between destination writing and listings, as well as a smattering of maps, with an inevitable metro map in city guides.

Thomas Cook Publishing (www.thomascook.com)

A guidebook publisher for 125 years, Thomas Cook produces six series. Hotspots (sixteen titles) cover popular resort destinations around the Mediterranean; Independent Travellers (seven titles) are budget guides for longer trips; Travellers (forty-nine titles) are compact colour guides; Welcome guides cover hotels, inns and B&Bs; and Must-See guides (eight titles) are for short-stay city travellers. Finally, the Signpost series is geared to self-drive holidays. Colour is abundant but the tone is pretty factual, with rating-systems taking the place of opinionated writing.

TimeOut (www.timeout.com)

London-based and part of the Penguin group along with Rough Guides, TimeOut produce fantastically comprehensive and sophisticated city guides, written and researched by resident journalists. Highlights include perceptive writing, objective reviews, fascinating sidebars and moody, predominantly black and white pics. Detailed colour maps cover mostly central areas – ideal for walkers. Though the cultural information is very satisfying, it's the attention to practical detail that impresses (a glance in the directory section turns up listings of English-speaking lawyers, couriers and relocation agencies). Covering thirty-three major cities, these in-depth guides are aimed at long-term visitors and new expats.

chapter 6: PACKING

Choosing the right luggage

There's no need to feel like a dork for travelling with a suitcase. Really. Backpackers may beg to differ, but a suitcase does not brand you a mere 'tourist' as opposed to a hip 'traveller'. If you're just doing the airport-taxi-hotel circuit, spending a fair stretch of time in just a couple of destinations, or headed for a resort holiday, a suitcase serves your needs just fine. Don't blow holiday spending money unnecessarily on a name-brand backpack. Definitely get a suitcase with wheels attached and, if your case is black, give it a distinguishing mark – such as a red sticker – in addition to a name tag.

However, if you're moving around a lot, a suitcase becomes a millstone. Suitcases travel well in tour buses and hire cars, but not on trains, trams and other local transport. On unpaved paths and the cobblestones of Europe, they are highly impractical. In smaller guesthouses and pensions, chances are you'll be hauling your case up flights of stairs. You may also find yourself forking out for taxis to take you just around the block to the train or bus station. And, of course, a suitcase only leaves you with one free hand, if that.

Gym bags, duffle bags or overnight bags with a shoulder strap are much easier to walk around with than a suitcase, though you may have to pack less. Wear the strap across your shoulder so you have both hands free, and make sure the bag can be locked, with either double zippers or handles that can be padlocked.

The more you travel, the more likely it is you'll own a backpack. Nothing beats their mobility and versatility. Backpacks and daypacks have become *de rigeur* – and with great popularity has also come trendiness and expense. At travel-equipment emporiums, you'll find state-of-the-art models mounted to the wall like rare butterflies, with price tags in excess of $1000. Extend your search to camping shops and army disposal stores. Unless you're on the move for months and expect your backpack to last a lifetime, there's no great need to pay for a top-of-the-line model.

For those who've never backpacked, travel packs are a good way to ease yourself into backpacker mode. With zippers that go around the top and sides and with stowaway handles, the travel pack can double as a suitcase. It saves you digging into the bottom of the pack to retrieve stuff, makes packing a snap, and is highly versatile.

The classic, top-loading backpack is more suitable for hikers, bikers and others who won't be changing their clothes three times a day. The disadvantage with these packs is ferreting out items from the bottom umpteen times a day. However, some models come with a separate bottom compartment or a zipper near the bottom of the pack so you can reach in there without unloading the whole thing.

A correct fit, of course, is most important. Make sure the size is right for you, with the pack neither too high nor too bulky. Either situation restricts your peripheral vision and mobility. Resist the urge to go for the biggest pack – consider not how much you can cram in but how much you can comfortably carry for long periods. Ask about models that come in male and female body shapes.

The back section is nearly always padded; check that the shoulder and waist straps are padded as well – this prevents the straps from cutting into you on days when you're carrying the pack for long hours. Check also that the weight is borne on your hips, not your shoulders, collarbone or back.

Ask for all the advice you can get from salespeople and start your search at least a couple of weeks before the trip. Fill the pack with clothes and books and give it a trial run at home. If it's uncomfortable, this is the time to return it. Buying a new pack in Europe, Japan or the US could inflict a mortal wound on the credit card.

Whatever your luggage, scrutinise the zips and fastenings. If these give out, the thing is useless. Strong zips and double stitching are all-important. The material should be durable, not too light, water-resistant and slash-proof. Finally, make sure that your luggage can be secured with a padlock.

Don't leave home without . . .

The more remote your destination, the more supplies you'll need to bring from home. If you're veering off the tourist track in Asia, Africa, Latin America and Eastern Europe, here's a list of items you shouldn't leave home without.

- **Bandaids and bandages:** you don't want to go searching for bandaids and pay for a whole packet when you only need a couple. Active travellers should also consider wound dressings for bigger mishaps.
- **Batteries:** put new ones in your camera, computer, alarm clock, radio, penlight, shaver, etc., and bring replacements.
- **Condoms:** quality varies around the world (check the production or use-by date) and they can be outrageously expensive in some places.
- **Contact lenses:** bring spares, and solution to soak them in.
- **Ear plugs:** for when you just have to get a few hours' sleep in a noisy hostel or bus.
- **Insect repellent:** assumes major importance in malaria-affected regions. Bring a trusted brand.

- **Maps:** in developing countries, don't assume you can buy detailed maps locally. Start your search at home and if you find a good map, take it with you.
- **Medication:** bring all your regular medication, including contraception, malaria antidote, etc., and all prescriptions.
- **Mosquito net:** for malaria-affected areas of Africa, Asia and Latin America. Many hotels provide nets but campers and other adventurers will need to bring their own.
- **Multivitamins:** nutrition quickly suffers when you're on the move and perhaps reluctant to eat local food for fear of getting sick. Vitamins are particularly good for lazy fruit and vegetable eaters.
- **Padlocks and small chains:** have a couple of spares on hand for all sorts of uses.
- **Phrasebooks:** these can be a lifesaver and locals will appreciate you for at least making an effort.
- **Pocket calculator:** for currency conversion.
- **Rehydration mixture:** for dehydration, especially from severe diarrhoea.
- **Sterile syringes and needles:** packs are available from travellers' clinics. A consideration if you

need a blood transfusion or injections in countries where medical facilities aren't the best.
- **'Stoppers' for diarrhoea:** antidiarrhoeals should be used only as a short-term measure. Useful on trekking trips, when you have to keep moving, and on long plane or overland journeys.
- **Tampons and sanitary pads:** supply and quality varies greatly. Bring your own.
- **Tissues:** a car or travel pack will suffice, to save your behind from the ghastly stuff that passes for toilet paper in some parts.
- **Toiletries:** bigger brands are available in most places, but if you're partial to a certain product, bring your own.
- **Water purification tablets or iodine:** for when tap water isn't safe to drink, and bottled or boiling water isn't a practical option.

Packing light

Overpacking is a real drag – something travellers often learn the hard way. A huge pack or suitcase tragically limits your mobility and the amount of travel you do. It also makes you a conspicuous target – a lone traveller struggling with a weighty suitcase is easy pickings for thieves, who often work in gangs.

Take more money and fewer clothes; shoes, toiletries and underwear are also far more important. Clothes can often be bought cheaply along the way. What was once strictly backpacker couture – khakis, polar fleece, cargo pants and shorts with practical roomy pockets – has become urban streetwear the world over, making it easy for travellers to blend in with the locals and to buy practical travel attire just about anywhere. The more you take, the bigger your laundry load. Here are some pointers for packing only what you need.

More time doesn't mean more clothes

Consider the activities you'll be doing, rather than the length of the trip. If you're sticking to one climate, you should pack the same for two months as you would for two weeks. It's the appropriateness of your clothing that matters, not the amount.

Co-ordinate or cull

Stick to one basic style and co-ordinate colours. If a jacket only looks good with a certain pair of pants or shoes, leave it. Everything has to work together.

Think layers
On the road, you'll often go from cool, early-morning starts to sightseeing in the heat of the day, to al fresco dinners. You need layers of clothing that you can peel off throughout the day. Take some singlets or T-shirts, long-sleeved tops, maybe a polar-fleece vest and heavier jumper or coat. Scarves, shawls, hats and gloves are great because they add a lot of warmth without the bulk. Limit bulky items to one or two. It's rare that you'll need a heavy jumper *and* a heavy coat. If you can't wear them together, do you really need both?

Naturals and neutrals
Natural fibres such as cotton and silk travel best because they can be cool or warm, they allow the skin to breathe, they absorb perspiration, tolerate hand or machine washing and can be worn several times between washes. Wool is also versatile but harder to take care of. All linens should be left at home. New synthetic materials geared for travellers

are hard-wearing, lightweight and dry in an instant but the better stuff is quite expensive. A combination such as stretchy cotton/lycra is great (though not in hotter climates) because you can throw it in a pack and it needs no hanging or ironing. Jeans are a travel must – black jeans are better because they can be dressed up and they don't fade or show grime as obviously as blue denim.

Dark neutrals are the best travelling colours – they are flattering, conservative, inconspicuous and they hide dirt and grime. For warmer climates, throw in some lighter colours such as off-white, sand and camel.

It's not about the clothes
Once you're on the road, your wardrobe assumes far less importance than seemed the case at home. Try to take on a traveller's mindset as you pack. Yes, you can (and will) wear the same clothes three days straight, although it's something you'd never contemplate at home or work. On the road, no one knows or is likely to care what you wore the day before. And most of the time, travel is so intoxicating that you feel fabulous in jeans and a singlet.

Feet first

One area of your wardrobe you should never skimp on is shoes. Being hobbled by ill-fitting or inappropriate shoes will make you miserable and cost you precious holiday time. You need three pairs max – three types, not colours. Your walking shoes/hiking boots will do most of the work, so get the best pair you can afford. A more refined pair will step out at restaurants and religious/cultural sites. Women should take a flat shoe or raised heel at most. Finally, for the beach, hot weather and shower blocks, pack a pair of thongs, sandals or rubber-and-velcro rafting shoes.

MUIs

Multiple-use items are beloved by travellers; take as many of these space savers as you can. Shorts are wonderfully versatile: you can hike in them, swim in them and sleep in them. A sarong or wraparound skirt is respectful attire for religious/cultural sights, a make-do sheet and a potential picnic rug. A pashmina shawl is both a practical warmer and an eye-catching accessory for a plain outfit. Depending on size, it can also be a travel throw or standby blanket. Dental floss can be used as washing line, security tie or emergency thread. Gaffer tape can be handy for packs and shoes that fall apart and also for taping valuables out of sight in your room. Jewellery is the opposite of a MUI – that is, useless. Leave it at home. Its only function on a trip is to make you an obvious target for thieves.

chapter 7: SAFETY

Keeping travel documents and money safe

Theft is the most common crime committed against travellers. Fortunately, most incidents are quick and opportunistic rather than calculated and violent. Study your destination. Know something about its crime rates and patterns, talk to locals or recent visitors and take the appropriate measures. Safety can be a major consideration if your destination is Johannesburg or Nairobi (aka 'Nairobbery') but far less of a concern in Japan or Korea, where theft and violent crime are rare.

You can never be theft-proof; the idea with all safety measures is to make it harder for thieves and force them to look for an easier target. Consider the image you present to a would-be thief. In general, avoid drawing attention to yourself with flashy jewellery, and bright, revealing or unusual clothes. In poorer places, a walkman or even a cheap watch can be an irresistible target. If you're carrying a bag, camera, computer or video equipment, hold it away from the street to deter drive- or ride-by snatch thieves.

At all times, try to look purposeful and alert. Avoid looking up at skyscrapers, pausing under street signs or anything else that identifies you as a tourist. An intoxicated, disoriented or distracted traveller is easy pickings. Even if you're lost, avoid rushing around in a panic with an open map or guidebook.

A money belt or neck wallet inside your clothes is the safest way to carry your passport and money. The former is a bit more comfortable and less visible. Money belts come in leather, synthetics (usually nylon) and cotton. Leather is the most durable but also the heaviest, and the sweat factor makes it uncomfortable in hot climates. Cotton is the most comfortable but needs washing. It also absorbs moisture so you'll need to protect your documents with plastic coverings. Synthetic belts can be bulky, and velcro fastenings announce to anyone within earshot that you're dipping into your cash supply. With all money belts, you'll need a smaller wallet or change purse to avoid regularly exposing your stash.

To and fro
Crowded transport hubs, especially train and bus stations, are where you are at most risk of theft. In Europe especially, gangs of thieves work these places, often with a distracting ruse such as thrusting newspapers in your face, bumping or jostling, or spilling something over you. If you feel startled, grab hold of your belongings.

On all public transport, keep a close eye on your gear. Consider carrying your pack in front on crowded trips, or chain it to a luggage rack. Daypacks are choice targets as their contents are obvious; put yours out of sight in your backpack or case and lock the bigger bag. When waiting for your bus/train, remember that newspapers and unfolded maps are great screens for thieves.

Night trains are far more risky, especially in eastern and southern Europe. Some locals suggest sewing your money into a shirt pocket; even then, you could well awaken to find your trouser pockets turned inside out. Avoid sleeping alone in an unlocked compartment. Secure or tape the door shut so that you'll be alerted if someone tries to enter.

On buses, it can pay to sit on the side of the baggage hold to observe other passengers when they alight. It certainly happens that locals who board a bus minus luggage make off with a tourist's bulky suitcase.

Back at your room

After transport, places of accommodation are the next most likely opportunity for thieves. The cheaper the accommodation, the greater the security risk. Unfortunately, the thief in this instance is likely to be a fellow traveller.

Don't always trust your room key; secure the door with your own padlock or some other means if possible. Stories abound of travellers unlocking their room door and finding strange luggage (or people) on the bed, only to realise they're on the wrong floor and one key fits all.

A locker or safe in your room shouldn't be

trusted unless you have your own means of locking it. A safe at reception is better – in theory – because it means the hotel/hostel will be liable for your losses. But this isn't much consolation in developing countries, where the hotel's insurance might only cover a fraction of what you lost. Sometimes, it's all the hotel can afford to pay; in more sinister cases, the hotel and even the local police can be in on the scam.

Honeymooners have often been targets of this type of theft, because of the wedding-present cash they carry, or are presumed to carry. Take only what you need; a pile of cash is too great a temptation in some parts.

In a dorm room, chain your backpack to the bed or some other solid fitting. Never leave your passport or money behind when you visit the bathroom. On weighing up the situation, you might want to take your whole pack into the bathroom. At night, put your money belt in the pillow case, or put your passport and money in a sock and sleep with it.

If your room is in a less-than-reputable guesthouse, give the impression that you're staying in.

Take your key with you rather than leave it at reception; turn a radio or TV on; or hang out the 'Do Not Disturb' sign when you go out. If you feel a break-in is likely, consider leaving out something – like a cheap wallet with a few notes and expired credit cards. Thieves rarely know how much time they have; they'll grab the obvious spoils and shoot through. Don't leave behind anything you can't bear to lose.

No matter if your accommodation is rated five-star or fallen star, be very wary of telling people where you're staying. Never give out your room number.

Hire cars

The world over, hire cars are all-too popular targets. They're easily identifiable and their drivers are presumed to have big cash reserves or expense accounts.

The best safety tip is never leave anything in the car, even if this means carting your stuff up several flights of stairs for an overnight stay of a few hours. Parking on the street in the centre of town, day or night, is asking for trouble. If you can, hire a sedan with a separate lockable boot, rather than a hatchback or stationwagon.

Leave nothing visible in the car; even a measly cassette can be an incentive for some thieves to wonder what greater riches lie inside. Some drivers, including locals, leave the glove box empty and open to show there's nothing inside to nick.

Be very suspicious if locals drive past and signal for you to pull over. If there's something wrong with the vehicle, chances are you'll know about it first. Wave them on; indicate that you're aware of the problem and will stop at the next filling station or town.

Out and about

Be vigilant at big, crowded sites and when shopping and eating. At outdoor cafés, never sling a bag over your chair. Keep your bag in your lap and your pack on the floor or ground, resting against your leg so you can detect anyone tampering with it.

Markets are a pickpocket's nirvana. It may be wiser to keep your pack in front. When trying on clothes, beware of hands reaching in to snatch your wallet or pack when you're half-dressed.

On the beach

Some travellers pull out the inner soles and keep money in their shoes at the beach. This isn't much use if you're wearing sandals or thongs. Nor is it safe if your footwear is a pricey pair of running shoes, which could be the target as much as the cash. Socks are another option. But there's no foolproof method at the seaside, where sole travellers are particularly vulnerable.

If you're with a partner, you may have to take it in turns to go swimming. If alone, you might weigh up the risks and give the swim a miss. Deserted stretches of beach anywhere are unsafe, especially for women.

A final word: paranoia about being robbed can actually rob you of good times, precious memories and contact with locals. Be alert but not anxious.

You should also recognise when robbery is the lesser of evils. Despite your best efforts, you could come up against an armed and desperate thief. Nothing in your pack is worth serious injury – or worse.

What to do in a legal emergency

Is an unscrupulous hostel owner holding your passport hostage? Were you car-jacked? Did you drop your pack in a foaming river miles from anywhere? Disasters and emergencies on the road are so varied and unpredictable that it's impossible to have a contingency plan for all crises. Nevertheless, some preparation is better than none. Imagine some worst-case scenarios and how you would deal with them.

First, avoid foreseeable legal trouble. Never take drugs into another country and never help new-found 'friends' by carrying bags and parcels for them. Check with your doctor or travel agent that any over-the-counter medication you plan to take is legal.

Make sure your passport and visa are in order. If you hold dual nationality, find out before leaving home whether your second country can call you up for military service or if it has any other 'claims' on you.

Some young women head overseas for family reunions, only to find themselves stripped of their passport and ticket, and forced into marriage. If you are at risk of this situation, ask consular services what your options are – both before and after the marriage.

If you're headed for a remote region, especially if you don't speak the language, take with you contact details of your country's nearest embassy. In places where there's no Australian diplomatic post, you might be able to call on British or Canadian embassies.

Find out beforehand exactly what the consul can do. For instance, your embassy can replace lost passports, call home to let relatives know your situation, arrange help with transferring money and issuing new tickets, and put you in touch with lawyers, interpreters and doctors. You may even get some money to tide you over. But don't expect a free plane ride back home. Consular services do not extend to investigating crimes, defending you in a legal matter, or moving you to a better hospital or place of detention.

Embassies also can't protect you from your own stupidity. If you get yourself in trouble by criticising foreign officials and governments, photographing military installations, drink-driving or taking part in illegal demonstrations, don't expect much sympathy.

If you are detained by authorities and remain truly baffled as to why, maintain a polite, respectful manner about the 'misunderstanding'. Be calm and persistent in asking for a phone call to let others know where you are. Give the authorities some room to back down gracefully. Aggressive, loud, pushy or rude behaviour, and ranting about incompetence or corruption will get you nowhere.

Always leave a copy of your itinerary with someone at home and check in with regular phone calls, faxes or emails. If you are going into arduous territory, let others – locally or at home – know when you expect to return. In an emergency, your first phone call should be to friends or relatives back home, who can contact the insurance company, embassy, etc., and arrange for money and other necessities to be sent to you.

For travellers in an isolated mountain village with no way to contact anyone, ask for a local doctor, teacher or village elder. Use a phrasebook if you have one, or indicate with diagrams and drawings that you need a telephone or some transport – a car, taxi, boat or plane. Draw your national flag, country map, or symbol – a kangaroo is unmistakable for Aussies. Once you've communicated where you're from, it may be easier to communicate what you need. Locals may realise, for instance, that you are an English-speaker and seek the same.

Hitchhiking

Hitchhiking is never safe in *any* country. Even supposedly hitcher-friendly countries such as Japan have their share of horror stories. Women travelling alone take the greatest risk; two women together aren't much safer. If you're relying on bumming lifts as a main form of getting around, it's a sign you haven't saved enough for the trip.

Nevertheless, plenty of travellers continue to hitch so it's important to know the different practices around the world. For instance, the thumb sign is not universally understood. In most parts of Africa and Asia, you simply wave down approaching cars and trucks.

Some hitchers display flags denoting their

nationality; this works better for some than others. A sign showing your destination is not advisable; drivers could claim they are also headed there to get you into the car. It's also a bad idea to throw your pack in the boot or anywhere else out of your sight. Don't get in a car if you sense bad vibes, especially if you suspect the occupants are intoxicated.

In many countries of Africa and Asia, some payment is expected. This could take the form of a gift – such as cigarettes or chocolate. In parts of Latin America, especially remote rural regions, private vehicles operate as de facto public transport, picking up locals and travellers along the way. A fixed-price fare usually applies.

Hitchhiking Cuban-style

Travellers are likely to see more hitchhikers in Cuba than any other country – with a twist. Chances are that you, the traveller, will be behind the wheel and the locals are the ones hitching.

The dreadful state of Cuban public transport, a dilapidated private fleet and the scarcity and expense of fuel means that hitchhikers are common roadside scenery in Cuba. You'll see everyone from soldiers to grandmothers waiting patiently for a car, truck or bicycle to slow down.

Stop to ask directions and chances are you'll have a local jump in the back seat and direct you to their home or place of work. Payment is rare; instead you'll have the pleasure of contact with locals, an invitation to drinks or dinner, or even a place to stay.

Foreigners who hitchhike in Cuba have plenty of competition but also the advantage of standing out from the crowd. Beware of locals who offer a lift, then claim their vehicle is an official taxi and charge ridiculous rates.

Women travelling alone

It's a reality that solo female travellers face more 'issues' than men. The more you know about the hassles in your particular destination, the better prepared you'll be to deal with them.

The most important rule for women travelling alone is to dress appropriately – you will be judged on your appearance whether you like it or not. Be aware of the local culture and what is considered appropriate attire. In more conservative Asian and Muslim countries, this entails covering up arms, shoulders and legs. Even in countries with heavy tourist traffic – such as Spain, Italy and Greece – you should dress more modestly away from tourist resorts, beaches, etc.

Women travelling alone attract much unwanted attention. Avoid drawing further scrutiny with bright, revealing or tight clothing, loud jewellery or a radical hairstyle. These could expose you to some appalling prejudices about Western women – namely, that your dress stamps you as 'fair game'.

Behaviour, too, should be quiet and conservative. A respect and understanding of local ways goes a lot further than a loud, argumentative manner. Beware of making waves. Shaking hands with men and holding eye contact may not be the done thing. You might think you have every right to be served in a café or bar but if these are male-only zones, you could be treated as a curiosity at best, or an object of abuse at worst.

Socialising with men can be like treading a minefield. Alcohol and the solo female traveller is not a good mix. Unless you are in a group, be wary of men who insist on buying you a drink. This can be seen as a green light for those with less than honourable intentions. In certain parts, be on guard against men slipping drugs into your drink. Make a point of paying for your own drink or saying no to the drink but yes to conversation.

If you're a woman travelling alone, avoid arriving in strange places at night, especially if you don't speak the language. Steer clear of lonely stretches of beach, night trains and empty compartments, badly lit streets and shortcuts through parks and side streets. Always have some cash on hand for a taxi fare. Hitchhiking is inadvisable, even for women travelling in pairs.

For a thorough treatment of female travel, see Rough Guides' *Women Travellers*, online at **www.roughguides.com**.

Alone in Austria

A woman travelling alone needn't spend the whole trip looking over her shoulder. Something about a female far from home can bring out the most kind and protective instincts in complete strangers.

Some years ago, I detached early from a tour group and spent a night at a hotel in southern Austria. Or rather half a night – I had to be on a railway platform at the ungodly hour of 4.15 a.m. to catch a train to Vienna and then the long flight back to Australia.

I was apprehensive about the train trip. The railway station wasn't in the glamorous part of town (is it ever?) and I wouldn't dream of catching a 4 a.m. train at home, let alone in a foreign town where my command of the local language extended to '*Sprechen sie English, bitte?*' Would I be alone on the platform – an easy target? Would desperate drunks be my only company? Should I stay awake and alert all night, or grab some sleep?

The hotel manager, a new immigrant from Hungary, sensed my unease and took me under his wing. Learning I was Australian, he called over his cousin Johnny who could converse more easily with me because he once lived in Melbourne. Then he 'liberated' a watermelon from the kitchen. We had a rooftop rendezvous and spent many pleasant hours under the stars, chomping on the fruit and listening to Johnny reminisce about St Kilda in the 1960s.

At 3.45 a.m., as agreed, the manager made the wake-up call. Downstairs he had the taxi waiting. We exchanged goodbyes like long-time friends and, just before I hopped into the car, he pressed sweets and gum into my hand for the long journey.

Sexual harassment

Sexual harassment is an annoyance you should prepare for in southern Europe, northern Africa, most of Latin America and parts of Asia, especially India and certain areas of Malaysia, Indonesia and the Philippines.

Single women are the most frequent victims of sexual harassment. Married women travelling alone may be accorded more 'hands off' respect in some parts. On the other hand, locals may consider you as good as single, since you're travelling without your spouse.

Harassment starts with low-level stares, provocative comments and woof-whistles – annoying but mostly harmless. Ignore it as much as possible and go about your business. A reaction of any kind is exactly what the tormentors are after, and acts as incentive to continue the offensive behaviour. Useful props include sunglasses to avoid eye contact and the old standby: a fake wedding band.

In countries where machismo rules, you may experience groping, pinching, etc. on public transport and in other crowded areas. How you respond depends on the local culture and situation. A sharp glare can be enough. The best response is usually a loud rebuke telling them to keep their hands to themselves. It's never really appropriate to whack the harasser.

Single women should link up with other travellers in threatening environments. Two women holding hands or linking arms can put off macho pests. The presence of a male companion will significantly cut down harassment. But not always. In parts of Asia or north Africa, for instance, local men may see it as a challenge to drag you away from a male partner – whether friend, boyfriend or husband. They can be brazenly upfront about it, or grab you as soon as your partner turns his back.

At its worst, sexual harassment extends to predatory behaviour, such as a tour operator who literally leads you up the wrong path on a trekking trip, or a hostel owner who enters your room at midnight just to make sure you're 'okay' and to help you turn down the bed. Where possible, remove yourself from situations like these and consider reporting the incident to help warn other travellers. Local police may not always treat these complaints seriously; try tourist offices, travel companies and travel guides who list the business, and even the local mayor or chamber of commerce. If harassment becomes assault, contact your embassy, which can help direct you in dealing with local police.

If you're headed for a country where the role of women is very prescribed (Pakistan, for example), consider seeking out a local women's organisation before you leave home. You'll probably get some excellent advice, and you'll have an important local contact and support if something goes wrong.

Gay and lesbian travellers

Gay and lesbian travellers should check their country of destination for anti-gay laws, especially in Asia, Africa and Latin America. Countries where homosexuality is illegal include Ecuador, India, Nicaragua, Pakistan and Singapore. Some countries have curiously conflicting laws – banning sex between males, but not lesbians, for example.

Even if the law accords equal status to gay people, the tolerance level in society may lag far behind. In general, you should exercise caution in being 'out and about'. Unless you're in gay-friendly territory, avoid public displays of affection. Men holding hands or linking arms is frowned upon in some places (e.g. southern Europe, Latin America), while two women doing the same would be puzzling in many parts of Asia. Depending on your destination, you may have to be creative when booking hotel rooms in person. The farther you venture from main cities, the more likely you are to encounter intolerant and homophobic attitudes.

Gay organisations are the best sources of information on the local gay scene. They offer reassurance and the opportunity to meet up with like-minded types. Many guidebooks list gay-friendly destinations, events and businesses; the Spartacus guides cater to gay travellers. See also gay-travel agencies and web sites, such as **www.gay.com**.

chapter 8: FLYING

Flying after 11 September

The airline industry worldwide suffered its biggest blow following the 11 September 2001 terrorist attacks on New York and Washington. Several airlines were permanently grounded in the last quarter of 2001 and others were driven almost to the wall by the public's fear of flying and travel. Tens of thousands of jobs were lost. For travellers, the impact of 11 September has resulted in the following changes to air travel.

- Increased pre-departure security checks. Arrive at the airport at least two hours before your flight. In the US, security is especially vigilant, so you may need to allow even more time, particularly if your departure point is a major air

hub – such as Los Angeles, Chicago, New York, Washington or Miami.
- More expensive airfares. The airlines' increased security and insurance costs have been passed down in the form of higher taxes on every sector that you fly.
- Severe restrictions on hand luggage. You can't overstate the sensitivity of airport security staff when it comes to potential weapons – as a champion boomerang thrower discovered in the US in mid-2002. Put in your check-in luggage any knives, bottle openers, letter openers, tweezers, nailfiles and nail clippers, even knitting needles. If dangerous items are detected after your luggage is on the plane, they will be confiscated.

Surviving long-distance flights

A long flight can take in many 'emotional zones' (not to mention time zones); everything from the exhilaration of take-off to sleepless exhaustion and claustrophic craziness at the end. A rough flight can wipe out the first day or so at your destination, which is particularly unfortunate if you're immediately hooking up with a tour or starting an arduous adventure holiday. Here are some tips to make the flight go more smoothly.

Before you fly

Well before you fly, call the airline to let them know of any special needs you might have – diet, disabilities, a travelling infant, etc. Airlines offer up to forty different meals, catering to all religious and dietary requirements. Some travellers request vegetarian meals purely for taste and because they are often better prepared than the standard fare. Airlines are also very helpful to people with disabilities – there are written announcements and information for the hearing-impaired, and assistance is readily available for people in wheelchairs.

For jet-setting infants, ask about the 'sky cots' and whether they can accommodate your child (the bassinets usually hold children weighing up to 10 kg). Some airlines allow you to wheel a pram onboard, provided it can be folded and the plane has the appropriate storage. Baby-friendly Qantas even provides baby food and nappies.

Many travellers don't bother reconfirming their flight three to five days before, but it's still recommended that you do so for peace of mind. Some airlines are notoriously overbooked and there is a possibility of being 'bumped'. It's an especially good idea to reconfirm when you're departing from a foreign country. Confirm both the airport (many cities have more than one) and terminal from where your flight departs. Take note of the reconfirmation number if you're given one. This is also a good time to remind the airline of any special requirements you have. For instance, if you're travelling with a small child, ask for a bulk-head seat (where the bassinets are) and if you can take a stroller as carry-on luggage.

On the day of travel

Travel agents can generally allocate plane seats when the ticket is purchased. If not, at check-in you will be issued a seat and boarding pass. Now's the time to sing out if you're hellbent on an aisle or window seat (both of these tend to fill fast). Window seats are for calm flyers who want to get some sleep, while aisle seats are preferred by those with itchy feet who like to get out of their seat a few times. For tall passengers, the bulkhead seats at the front of each section and the exit-row seats have more leg room.

Clothing should be loose and comfortable but still presentable. Remove belts and ties, and perhaps also your shoes, as feet tend to swell inflight. Replace contact lenses with glasses on long flights.

Drink plenty of water and juice to alleviate dehydration in the dry, pressurised cabin air. Bring your own large (two litre) bottle of water and be sure to finish it on the flight. Avoid excessive amounts of alcohol and caffeine – they contribute to dehydration, bring on headaches (hangovers and migraine) and interfere with sleep.

For the lucky few who can sleep, a window seat, travel pillow and earplugs seem to do the trick. Avoid sleeping pills as you don't want to arrive in a drowsy state; in many cases, drug-induced sleep is far from truly restful.

Avoid staring at the seat in front. Busy yourself with writing, reading your travel guide or other books, studying your phrasebook, listening to music and watching films. Move around the cabin a few times and spend at least five minutes in every hour moving and stretching your legs and arms (see the DVT section below for more suggestions).

All the physical preparations are useless without the right attitude. Accept that you'll be in that seat a long time. Curl up and get as comfortable as possible. Fidgeting, complaining, watching the clock compulsively or eating and drinking excessively won't make the flight go any faster.

DVT

When Australian cricket captain Steve Waugh developed Deep Vein Thrombosis (DVT) in 2001, it was a sober reminder that even elite athletes are not immune to the condition. Waugh's story followed several well-publicised cases, some of them fatal.

DVT is the formation of a blood clot, usually in the legs, which can travel up the body and block arteries around the heart or in the lungs or brain. DVT is a risk when flying because it can be caused by prolonged inactivity.

Sitting in a plane for long periods strains the back, stiffens muscles, compresses major blood vessels in the legs and restricts circulation — hence the swollen feet and ankles experienced on long flights. The lack of blood flow back to the heart causes swelling and risk of clotting in the lower body.

Activity greatly reduces the chances of developing DVT inflight. Moving the feet and legs for several minutes every hour – or only about 10 per cent of the time – is the best precaution.

Follow the exercises on the inflight video or in the inflight magazine and make sure you get out of your seat a few times and walk around the cabin.

Risk factors for DVT include: a family history of blood clotting; blood disorders that result in clotting; heart problems; obesity; smoking; pregnancy; advanced age; recent surgery; dehydration; and varicose veins. If you have two or more of these conditions, talk to your doctor before the trip. You could be given blood-thinning medication, compression stockings or other means to prevent swelling of the legs.

Contact your airline if you need more information or reassurance. Qantas has a section on DVT (including an inflight workout with diagrams) on its web site. Go to: **www.qantas.com.au**.

Travel sickness

It's rare these days to see a fellow passenger barfing into their sick bag. Nonetheless, travel sickness is no joke; combined with jet lag and huge climate change, it can lay you low for some time.

Travellers who are terrified of flying should visit their doctor. If information and reassurance don't do the trick, the doctor may prescribe or suggest a medication to help you relax. Those who don't want the drowsiness associated with this type of medication can opt for herbal remedies. Ask for these at your local health store.

Air turbulence can make white-knuckle flyers out of us all. If the weather is clear, focus on a stable object such as the sun or stars or the horizon if in view. Motion sickness is caused by a conflict between our sense of vision and our equilibrium (from movement of fluid in the inner ear). Focusing on a stable object helps – though admittedly, this can be hard to do on a shuddering plane.

Those who suffer from travel sickness should avoid staring at the seat in front. Try for a bulkhead seat (the front row of each section) as you'll have no one in front and you can concentrate on the video screen. In general, go for a seat nearer the front of the plane so you're not looking at a sea of headrests before you.

Drink plenty of water and don't overeat; perhaps ask ahead for a light vegetarian meal if you feel queasy on a plane.

Lost luggage

Minimise the impact of losing your luggage by taking all necessities in your hand luggage. This should already include your passport, ticket, all other travel documents (for example, your itinerary), money and money belt. Add all essential medication, glasses or contact lenses plus solution, basic toiletries (toothbrush, toothpaste and facewasher), plus your address book, camera, guidebooks and ideally a change of clothes.

Ensure each piece of luggage is marked with your name, a contact address and phone number and perhaps the airline you're flying with. It's also good to add a distinguishing feature such as a red sticker or tie around the handles.

When checking-in your luggage, make sure

the correct destination tags are attached. Don't be scared to ask 'dumb' questions (such as, 'Is "CDG" the correct airport code for Paris?'). At least you'll get a reassuring answer. ('Yes, Charles de Gaulle airport.') If you're changing flights, ask whether your bags will go straight onto the connecting flight (most likely) or if you need to collect them and check-in again. Ask if a baggage-claim slip is required. Some airports won't allow you to exit with bags unless you produce the claim slip.

If you're the lonely last at the baggage carousel and still without your luggage, don't panic. Head for the lost-luggage desk and make a report. Airlines do their utmost to find and return lost luggage, often far more quickly than you'd expect. Give it about 24 hours; in cases of mistaken bag swapping, the person who made off with your bag may not even realise it for several hours. Of course, this can be a major hassle if you're due to join a tour group. This is another reason to allow at least a day or two at your first stop before kicking off your trip. Once a couple of days have passed with no word, you should report your baggage as stolen. Make a police report and contact your insurance company.

Staying sane during flight delays

Like long queues and inedible airline food, flight delays are an inevitable part of the travel experience. Ask frequent travellers how best to pass the time and the most popular response is: 'Go get smashed in the lounge.' The lounge, at least, is a good idea.

Those of us who don't have access to these well-stocked sanctuaries can ask at the airport information desk about available facilities. Some airports have great amenities, with showers, fitness areas (for jogging) and even nap rooms.

If your terminal-cum-detention-centre lacks these luxuries, it could be a good opportunity for letter or journal writing. Bookshops and foreign newspapers will also help pass the hours.

The most original pastime comes from a globetrotting writer who stays sane by eavesdropping on other people's conversations! The less brazen among us can simply enjoy the passing parade.

chapter 9: ON ARRIVAL

Orientating yourself at your destination

Once you've found and settled into your accommodation, the best way to orientate yourself to the new surroundings is to take a long walk through the area and get a feel for the lay of the land. Note directions, the names of main streets and the location of nearby landmarks, restaurants and cafés, bus and train stations, post offices, banks, supermarkets, laundrettes, etc. If you're in a large town, try to get your hands on a map – even a sketch map from a tourist office will help give you a mental picture of the town layout.

Taking in the sights of your first destination when you're fresh off the plane is one of the most stimulating parts of the whole trip, particularly if it's your first time in Asia, Europe, the African bush, etc. Just drink it all in – the climate, people, sounds and smells.

For Aussies, New Zealanders and Britons, a trip anywhere outside these countries means a big adjustment when it comes to crossing the road, as much of the rest of the world drives on the right. Seems simple but it does take some getting used to. Take special care crossing at big intersections. Aussie drivers and pedestrians are involved in many near misses abroad, or worse.

Jet lag – that strange sensation of having your body-clock in another time zone – makes it tough to adjust to your new surroundings. If you arrive during the day, do all you can to hold off sleep until evening. Taking a good long walk clears the head, stretches the legs and gives you incentive to stay awake rather than crash into a jet-lagged slumber in the middle of the afternoon.

If you're negotiating a dramatic climate change – from an Australian summer to a wintry Europe, or going from winter to steamy South-East Asia – opt for a couple of shorter walks rather than one long hike. Avoid sensory overload on your first time out – this is basically a 'reconnaissance' trip to set you up for the days ahead.

Changing money

Changing money will be at or near the top of your 'to do' list. For countries with convertible currency, try to bring some local cash from home. This can be very handy if your flight arrives at 1 a.m. local time, when all the foreign-exchange outlets at the airport are closed. Just bring enough for one night's accommodation, food and a taxi fare. Do some homework on your destination. Some countries have very restrictive currency laws, allowing only about $50 in local currency to be taken in or out of the country.

Airports are rarely the best places to change money but you may have little choice. If you arrive on a Saturday night or Sunday, or on the eve of a national holiday, it's definitely worth changing a small amount to tide you over until you can get to a bank.

Avoid using ATMs at night, especially if you're on your own and have just arrived in a strange city. It's best to wait until the morning. They are obvious targets for thieves, and in many countries ATMs do not operate around the clock. Even in Japan, many close at around 9 p.m.

Avoid moneychangers on the street. This practice is far more 'kosher' in some countries than others, but basically if something goes wrong, you have no recourse. The local police and the companies providing your traveller's cheques and insurance won't appreciate your dabbling in the black market. Head for large banks in the centre of town, which usually offer the best rates. Compare the rates at a few places. There may be little fluctuation, but at other times you could save yourself a bundle.

Be aware that places that advertise cheap rates often do not include their fees in the promotion. You may need to weigh up a higher rate with no commission versus a lower rate with high fees to decide which is the better deal. Before handing over any traveller's cheques, be sure that the fee is per transaction, rather than per cheque.

If the staff at a bank don't speak English, write down the amount you want, expressed in the local currency if possible. In expensive countries – Western Europe, Scandinavia, Japan, the US – go for big bills. In developing countries, most of your cash should be in small bills.

Dealing with culture shock

Culture shock describes a range of feelings – fright, revulsion, frustration, anger – experienced by travellers after plunging into a culture alien to their normal environment. The differences can be so confronting that you feel unable to function or participate in the local culture. Homesickness is not culture shock, although it certainly fuels the feelings of dislocation, confusion and alienation. It's natural to yearn for the familiar when you're bombarded with the new, strange and foreign.

Even experienced travellers can suffer from culture shock. Little wonder. You step off a plane and all of a sudden a completely different world is in your face: a changed (usually oppressively hot) climate; shocking volumes of noise, people and pollution; and, in some places, desperate poverty. Food is unfamiliar or unappetising. All street signs are indecipherable, and you're rendered mute by your inability to speak the language. You could be disturbed at seeing child exploitation or animals slaughtered in the street. In predominantly black Africa, and in many parts of the developing world where tourists are few, Westerners are relentlessly (but not threateningly) stared at.

Fortunately, this sense of being overwhelmed will pass. Culture shock has several stages. At first, you are enthralled by all you see. Then you may become angered, revolted and frustrated at the difficulty of it all – this is when you retreat to your room and vow never to re-emerge. Inevitably you do, and gradually you'll find some positives to put in the picture. With confidence restored, you'll venture out and explore independently. Finally, you engage with the culture and gain some true appreciation for local ways.

Culture shock is not preventable but some preparation will help ease its impact. Read up before your trip, especially about the people you'll be meeting. The more informed you are, the better. Sleep can be a good remedy. The shock and bewilderment on arrival, when you are exhausted from a long flight, can ease considerably after a good night's rest. Once you've allowed yourself some time to adjust, try to interact with local people, rather than stand back. Here, language skills are all-important; just a few words can be the key to engaging with the society.

Build some adjustment time into your itinerary. Don't do any major 'cultural immersion' activities on the first or even second day. Give yourself some refuge from the deluge. If you feel assaulted by noise levels, stay in a better hotel to ensure you get proper rest. Have an occasional break from local street food – splurge on a meal at a more up-market restaurant or hotel.

Culture shock can be especially hard for solo travellers. If several days have elapsed and you're still miserable, a drastic change to the itinerary may be required. You might have to accept that Bangladesh was an ambitious first destination and head for somewhere less confronting, such as Thailand or Malaysia.

Acclimatising

Hopping between continents and time zones can feel like you're in the twilight zone. The first step in acclimatising is adjusting to time changes and the disruption to sleep patterns. On the first day, do all you can to avoid going to sleep during the day – admittedly a lot easier said than done. Unpack, go for a walk, change some money and get your bearings. Keep the first couple of days low-key and save the big cultural events and sights for after you've settled in.

Get involved in activities rather than walk around with a camera all day. Cycling, shopping at local markets or visiting a bathhouse are fun, relaxing ways to access the local culture and its people.

Don't be afraid to try the local food; this is a big part of acclimatising to new surroundings. Restaurants with high local and traveller turnover should be safe. Leave the more exotic fare for a bit later in the trip – there's no need to try haggis, roasted guinea pig or fried scorpions on the first day.

Make an effort to communicate with locals. A few key phrases can make all the difference. Ask about their favourite spots and nearby places of interest. Also ask about their family and background. Bring out any wallet pictures you may have of family members, pets or your house.

Meeting locals and other travellers

Meeting fellow travellers is a lot easier than avoiding them. Unless your destination is outer Mongolia, you'll be crossing paths with hordes of travellers, most of them bursting with newly acquired experience and advice.

In backpacker ghettos such as Khao San Road in Bangkok or Thamel in Kathmandu, you'll literally be tripping over travel packs. Other traveller meeting points include hostel kitchens and laundrettes, ferries, trains and buses, major sights, Internet cafés and visa queues at embassies. On the road, it's amazing how your ears become attuned to a home accent at a hundred paces. Travellers love to swap stories and tips, so you'll not lack for interaction if you want it.

Locals you are likely to meet include tourist office workers, guides, drivers, and staff at hotels, cafés and bookshops. Renting a room or apartment from locals is a good opportunity for conversation and a closer relationship. Locals give you an 'in' to a culture that no guidebook can.

If you're camping in rural, remote areas of

Asia, Africa and Latin America, chances are a welcoming party will come out to greet you. You might end up playing football, having your hair braided or being asked to perform or join in a song and dance session. All without speaking the language!

Men should be careful about initiating contact with local women, other than tourism workers and women in official positions. Some cultures disapprove of local women shaking hands, conversing or even holding eye contact with foreign men.

Making the most of your time and location

Walk to see the detail. Many ancient cities were designed for walking. Even in a wintry Europe, provided there's no wind chill and you're dressed appropriately, it's quite comfortable walking around.

Get out of tourist ghettos. A tour of monuments, museums and great shopping streets gets sterile very quickly. Museum fatigue can set in before the first exit sign. A big lure of travel is seeing how other people live – this also makes you feel more connected to a place. Ask hotel workers, taxi drivers, shop and restaurant staff where locals go to relax.

When in Rome . . . fall in with local rhythms. In southern Europe during summer and in places with hot, tropical climates year-round, the streets are deserted in the afternoons, when locals take a couple of hours' siesta – for good reason. Don't plan anything arduous for the afternoons in these places.

At major tourist attractions, get an early start to beat the crowds. This might entail being at the gate even before opening time. You'll enjoy these places so much more if you haven't had to queue for an hour and jostle your way through. Avoid weekends when locals throng to popular sights as well. Don't miss a festival or other cultural event that your trip coincides with.

Budget travellers often travel at night to save money on accommodation. The downside, however, is bigger: there is less safety at night and you don't get to appreciate the changing scenery – a major reason for travelling overland. Enjoy the journey, not just the destination.

Consider what you enjoy doing, rather than just tick off a long list of 'must-sees'. Drop out of a tour group if you're not getting anything out of it. You may do better on your own. Some tours presume no knowledge of local culture and can be boring or downright patronising.

chapter 10: CULTURAL PROTOCOL

General tips on cultural issues

Fearing extreme embarrassment or 'social death' in a foreign society is understandable when you don't have the cultural keys. Fortunately, as a visitor, you will almost always be cut some slack. And you can avoid obvious social bloopers by observing closely the behaviour of locals and by following some basic rules of cultural protocol.

Most important is to dress modestly. Be neat and presentable at important cultural sites and when dealing with officials – at embassies and police stations, in customs queues and the like. This demonstrates respect for the local culture and ensures you'll be treated seriously. Grimy, shabby or ripped clothes are offensive in places where the locals, albeit poor, go to great efforts to look their best in the few clothes they do own. Cover up away from beaches and resorts. Men in shorts are objects of ridicule in some countries, where short pants are worn only by local schoolboys.

Displays of anger, impatience and rudeness are unacceptable everywhere. So too criticism of a country's religious and cultural practices and its government. You'll gain more from listening rather than lecturing. Also, throughout the Third World and other socially conservative societies, avoid public displays of affection, whether between the opposite sex or same sex.

Ethnicity and religion are highly sensitive issues in culturally diverse and disputed regions. Be careful when identifying people by nationality. Don't assume that everyone in Russia is Russian. Be wary of identifying Slovaks or their language as 'Czech'. In Croatia, don't call the language 'Serbo-Croatian'. A history of war and occupation can leave lingering hostility between neighbours. Koreans, for example, will not appreciate you pointing out similarities with Japanese culture.

Be especially observant of local custom and

behaviour at cultural and religious sites. Dress conservatively and speak quietly. At sacred Buddhist, Hindu and Muslim sites, you are usually required to take off your shoes. Women may be required to cover their hair before entering a mosque. Scarves for this purpose are often available for visitors. So too are yarmulkes for men entering synagogues. At Buddhist temples, do not point at images of Buddha, especially with your feet, which should face away. In Hindu temples, where the cow is sacred, you will need to leave outside anything made of cow leather, such as bags, belts and shoes.

Show respect for religious practice. Don't expect a tour of a mosque on a Friday. At places of worship, you may be refused entry to the main hall, especially during prayer times. Women may be refused entry altogether. Lastly, always ask permission before taking photos.

Away from the all-business culture of the West, you will be expected to engage in greetings rituals and other forms of social lubrication. Upon entering a café or shop, for instance, you should greet the proprietor and also acknowledge them when leaving. At a minimum, you should learn local greetings, how to say yes, no, please and thank you. This small effort on your part can make a surprisingly big impact. Do not launch into English and expect to be understood. You should at least preface your question by stating that you don't speak the local language, or by asking people if they speak English.

Directness, considered a virtue in the West, can be seen as downright rude elsewhere. Always greet someone personally before launching into your questions. Shaking hands when meeting people and again when leaving is *de rigeur* in many non-Western countries. This may not apply to women, however. Take your cue from locals. Men should be careful about approaching local women in traditional societies.

Always ask permission before taking someone's photo, especially during cultural events, weddings, etc. Locals in areas of heavy tourist traffic may expect payment for this. Often, a copy of the photo is all the reward they want.

Throughout Asia, do not point at people, especially with your feet (so that people can see the sole of your shoe). Also, do not beckon in the usual

Western way, by wiggling fingers with the palm facing upwards. This gesture is viewed as vaguely offensive to obscene. The local way is to move the fingers with the palm facing down.

In many parts of Asia and Africa, refrain from publicly using the left hand to eat, touch others or receive items. In these countries the left hand is reserved for toilet duty.

If you are invited home, remove your shoes at the door, unless your hosts say otherwise. Bring a gift such as flowers, chocolates or wine. When buying blooms, you may want to check that they are not funeral flowers. Westerners are objects of intense curiosity in the developing world, so be prepared to answer all manner of questions that would be considered personal or intrusive at home. For example: How much do you earn? Why aren't you married? Why are you childless? Why are you travelling without your spouse?

When asking for directions outside the West, it pays to ask a couple of different people. In some cultures, providing an answer (even if it's way off track) is considered the polite thing to do. It's also a form of saving face. Locals believe it does not reflect well on them if they have to admit to an outsider that they don't know their own turf.

If negotiating local customs will occupy a big part of your trip, take a look at the Culture Shock! series which is devoted to customs and etiquette. These demystifying and entertaining guides are especially useful if you're moving abroad to live, or simply need more in-depth coverage of local culture than the standard guidebook provides. The Culture Shock! series numbers about sixty titles, from Argentina to Vietnam.

Dealing with the police

Do all you can to avoid dealing with police. Be sure your travel documents are in order. Do not take photos of police or military personnel or facilities. Even when your patience is severely tested by local bureaucrats, don't lash out with accusations of corruption or incompetence. Never fall for the temptation of buying cheap drugs overseas, or offering to carry parcels for newly acquainted fellow travellers.

If you should find yourself in custody, don't

pretend you know the law better than the local police. Also don't assume you can bribe your way out of trouble. Politeness, respect and even good humour will go far. Playing the 'dumb foreigner' during instances of 'misunderstanding' can also help. Police want you to see that they're the boss. Acknowledge their authority and give them room to back down gracefully in letting you off. The worst thing you can do is lose your cool. Stay calm and politely insist on a phone call to let others know where you are.

Toilets around the world

Toilet humour is bound to feature in many of your travel stories after the trip – make that *well after* the trip! Recalling contenders for the world's worst toilet is funny only in hindsight.

The good news for Westerners is that if you're sticking to the beaten path and staying in mid-range or better hotels and guesthouses, chances are you'll be sitting down to business in the little room. However, the Western-style toilet doesn't always come with a toilet seat. Nor does it come with Western plumbing. Throughout Latin America, most of Asia and Africa and parts of southern and eastern Europe, the plumbing system cannot cope with toilet paper, so use the bin that's normally provided. In these parts, you should also carry your own supply of toilet paper. Don't expect all sit-down loos to come with toilet paper, either, although it's readily available at supermarkets or grocery stores.

For the exotic toilet experience, you're looking at the squat variety – usually a hole in the ground with planks or raised sections for your feet. These are the norm in Asia and Africa, rural areas of Latin America and dilapidated public facilities in eastern and southern Europe. At the latter, you may see attendants selling squares of paper – this is your fee for using the toilet. Elsewhere, you'll see a water supply in a bucket with a bowl or jug nearby. Keep it handy. This is for washing yourself (while still squatting over the toilet) and then for flushing the waste.

Some travellers adjust pretty quickly to the squatting technique; others never do. Beware of glasses, wallets and change falling out of trouser or shirt pockets into deep, dark cacca-holes.

Normally you squat facing the door; Japan is the exception. Also in Japan, at homes and traditional guesthouses, you may find a pair of toilet slippers just near the door. Don't forget to remove them on exiting the toilet.

Other toilet types include long-drops or pits, either with or without a seating arrangement. You'll find these in the African bush – sometimes with great views – or in parts of the Himalayas where the toilet room hangs over the edge of a building. The worst toilets are normally East–West hybrids, such as an excrement-covered toilet bowl, minus running water, placed over a pit.

Trekkers who use the great outdoors as their toilet should bring a trowel as well as toilet paper. Bury waste well away from tracks and streams. A pen-torch can come in handy for answering calls of nature at night.

Scarcity of public toilets is another issue altogether. Make the most of better facilities at hotels and guesthouses. Airports and bus and train stations normally have toilets, though in remote areas they can be truly awful. Throughout Latin America, polite requests to use restaurant or café restrooms are rarely refused. In other places, you'll have to buy something to pay for the privilege. McDonalds outlets are a favourite option, though increasingly you might find the restrooms locked. On long bus journeys in South America or Africa, you may find yourself at impromptu toilet stops. For women travellers, long skirts are best for preserving some privacy and modesty.

For highly informative and amusing toilet talk, including a comprehensive listing of free and whistle-clean public toilets the world over, visit **www.thebathroomdiaries.com**.

chapter 11: PLANNING YOUR DAYS

When your time away is limited

Everybody travels differently. Some like the certainty of a structured itinerary – knowing where they're going, what they're doing and when. Other travellers enjoy a more laid-back and spontaneous approach, just seeing what comes up.

If your time is very limited, you need to do some planning to get the most out of a trip. This needn't be a rigid and oppressive schedule covering every hour of the day. It's more of a time-saver so that you can devote your energy to savouring the best bits at your destination.

First, study your destination. Pore over your guidebook before you arrive so that you're ready for a frontal assault as soon as you land. Second, consider pre-booking accommodation so that you don't waste precious hours shuttling between hotels and guesthouses.

If you have just two or three days in a highlights-packed place such as Paris, you'll need to make a list of the must-sees and then be selective. One or two major sights during the day is enough. If you've come a long way, don't do anything too arduous or culturally confronting on the first day. Ease into your new surroundings.

At vast European art museums, *don't even try* to see it all. You'd need a week. Instead, choose an area of interest and concentrate your energies there. You'll get much more out of these places if you can avoid museum fatigue.

At tourist offices and some hotels and guesthouses, ask for local guides or drivers who can facilitate travel and entry into attractions, especially if you don't speak the language. This not only saves a lot of travel time but gives you local perspective and company.

Consider using the most efficient form of transport if you're a short-stay visitor. Negotiating the local metro or bus system will be cheaper than taxis, but it could cost you a lot in terms of sights unseen.

If you're hitting Europe or North America in the peak summer season, you need to plan and pre-book a good part of your accommodation and activities, or else spend hours in queues. Get an early start at the most popular attractions, before the crowds and heat descend. Ditto in the tropics, where you should plan to rest in the afternoon. Everyone else will be.

Remember to include activities that you enjoy. This is more important than ticking off a must-do list of attractions. Cycling, jogging, rollerblading, playing tennis and going to a market can all be exhilarating in a foreign locale. The most memorable moments of a trip are usually unplanned and unlikely to involve major sights. You're more likely to reminisce about your dinner in the home of an Indian family; jogging through an eerily foggy and deserted Venice Beach; or crossing the Charles Bridge and catching your breath at the sight of Prague Castle shrouded by a golden sunset.

Finally, don't hesitate to scale down your itinerary if all you are getting out of it is exhaustion.

Take a day off if you need it, and sit around the pool reading or talking to other travellers. Remember – the faster you move, the less you absorb.

chapter 12: LANGUAGE

Making yourself understood

Despite what some travellers say, it isn't true that 'everybody speaks English'. This may be the case in northern and much of Western Europe, as well as the Indian subcontinent. In Africa, the sixteen countries that were once British colonies have English as the official or second language. English-speakers also abound in tourist enclaves of Morocco and Tunisia. But English alone won't get you far in eastern Europe, Asia and Latin America.

Even in countries where some English is spoken, the farther you venture from major centres and the older the locals, the less likely it is English will be understood. So you could well find yourself struck mute at some point in your trip. For this reason, independent travellers really should invest in a phrasebook, two-way dictionary or at least a guidebook with a basic language section. Even if you don't plan to learn great slabs of a phrasebook, it can be extremely useful if you've strayed way off the beaten track.

Minus phrasebook, you can try gesturing or drawing diagrams. People may be more comfortable in your presence and willing to help if they know where you are from. Try drawing your country outline, national symbol, flag and the like. For a toilet, many cultures understand the 'WC' abbreviation.

It would be a pity and a big mistake to let your lack of language mean a lack of interaction with locals. Smiling is a universal language. In rural parts of Africa, children might greet you and want to touch your straight hair or freckled skin. Singing, dancing and sport are also great ways to interact with people of other cultures.

Learning a bit before you go

Even for the linguistically gifted, languages vary in difficulty, from the relatively simple Spanish or

Bahasa Indonesia to the daunting Hungarian, Japanese or Mandarin. Regardless of the language, there's no doubt that speaking even a mangled version of the local tongue is a huge advantage for travellers. Not only does it enable you to board the right train and order something recognisable at restaurants, it gives you an 'in' to the culture. Conversing with locals is cultural immersion at its best.

When it comes to learning languages, a small effort invariably brings a big pay-off. Locals will greatly appreciate your interest in their language. You should make an effort to learn basics such as:

>   Good morning/Good day/Good evening/
>   Good night
>   Hello and goodbye
>   Please and thank you
>   Sorry/Excuse me/Pardon me
>   Help
>   I'm lost
>   Where is the toilet/bank/post office/doctor/
>   chemist/market/police station?

142 TRAVEL TIPS

>Where do I catch the train/bus/tram/taxi/boat?
>How much does this cost?
>Do you speak English?
>I do not speak . . .
>I do not understand
>I am from . . .
>Can you help me?

Self-motivated learners swear by audio tapes, but these do require discipline. Attending language classes, either at a university, cultural institute or language school, provides structure and classmates to practise with. You could also post a message at a university language faculty asking for a final-year student to tutor you. This will be cheaper than a commercial language school, and you have the benefit of concentrated one-on-one learning. Also, you can decide when, where and how many classes you want.

Whatever the method of learning, you should also expose yourself to the language as much as possible. Watch films and TV shows, listen to music and attend restaurants so that you can learn to order your favourite dishes on the trip. All these activities will add to your knowledge and confidence.

Both from a practical and cultural viewpoint, language will broaden your travel experience. Do make the effort to learn a few useful phrases and words. You won't regret it.

Language courses overseas

Depending on the length of your stay, you may want to enrol in a language course at your destination. These can vary from two-week intensives to several months of study. Costs also vary greatly, from several hundred dollars for a full-time short course, to several thousands for months of nightly or weekly classes. At short courses, accommodation (a homestay, university dorm or student hostel) and full board is normally included. This provides a great hit of local culture, and you have the benefit of immediately putting your learning to the test.

National tourist offices (in your country) and regional tourist offices abroad are the best places to start your enquiries (go to the Tourism Offices Worldwide Directory at **www.towd.com**). So too cultural institutes such as Alliance Française, the

Italian Cultural Institute and the German Goethe Institute. These are likely to be more helpful than dealing directly with foreign universities or embassies. Other good options are specialty-travel operators such as AmeriSpan Unlimited (www.amerispan.com), which offers Spanish-language packages throughout Latin America. Also try searching the Internet for the language you're after.

For the more popular European languages, such as French, Italian, Spanish and German, start your course research early, especially if you're arriving in the peak summer season. Some countries – Italy and Korea, for instance – require foreign nationals enrolled at a university or language school to obtain a study visa, which is normally issued only for the duration of the course. You will need to provide proof of enrolment and sufficient funds to last your stay. Also, the school might have to be government-approved in order to get the visa.

chapter 13: TRANSPORT

Negotiating local transport

Riding on local transport can be a blast. You know you're in Japan when you're riding in a bullet train, or in Venice as you cruise the canals in a gondola or vaporetto. In many developed countries, little 'negotiation' of local transport is required; you'll marvel at the humming efficiency of systems that move masses of people like clockwork. In developing countries, perhaps as you wend and weave through heat, humidity and heavy traffic in a bicycle rickshaw, you'll marvel at the organised chaos of a sea of humanity flowing in a million directions.

Transport around the globe is tremendously varied. Generally, your options will be airplane, train, tram, bus, taxi (including tuk-tuks and rickshaws of South-East Asia), bicycle and boat. In Western countries, your choice of transport will come down to factors of cost, efficiency and convenience. In the Third World, safety and comfort will figure more in your considerations.

For the intricacies of public transport in specific countries, the best sources of information are guidebooks, tourist offices, public transport offices, train stations, some travel agents and other travellers. Here are some general tips.

- Familiarise yourself with the 24-hour clock, which most transport timetables use.
- Large transport hubs can have several airports and train stations. New York City has three international airports. Paris has six mainline train stations; Vienna has three. Many cities have several bus stations, depending on the routes they service. When booking or confirming a flight, confirm the airport and terminal as well. Check the station name on train and bus tickets. Don't assume that your connecting ride departs from the same station. You could be looking at a hop across town. On arrival, you could find yourself kilometres from the hotel

to which you had planned to walk.
- In Europe, many major attractions are within walking distance of a metro stop. Grab a metro map and study it – chances are the metro will be your main form of transport. Familiarise yourself with the major lines – colours, numbers, names (usually the last station on the line) and also the transfer stations. Keep the map with you to check that you're going in the right direction. If you can't read or speak the local language, you won't be able to rely on signs and station announcements.
- Trains are generally safer and more comfortable than buses, though buses are almost universally cheaper and cover territory not serviced by train. In regions without an extensive rail network, such as Africa and Latin America, most overland travel is by bus. This could take the form of a sleek air-conditioned coach, a crammed minibus or a glorified truck.
- Trains and buses normally come in three types: express (few if any stops); semi-express (a few stops at major centres); and local (stopping everywhere). These can also be

expressed as direct, semi-direct or regular. Ticket prices are set accordingly; that is, depending on the duration, not distance, of the trip. The price difference can be negligible. Unless you consider it a priceless experience to spend eighteen hours crossing the Andes in a rattling bus with chickens and pigs as fellow passengers, it's worth the few extra dollars to trade up.

- Classes of bus or train depend on the amenities. In India, no less than five classes of bus await the traveller, everything from air-conditioned, video-equipped luxury coaches to rust buckets that look like something out of *Mad Max*. Trains normally offer three classes of carriage. In Europe, North America or Japan, first-class is an extravagance; second-class, usually with air-conditioning and reclining seats or compartments, is perfectly comfortable. In India, China or Africa, third-class can mean no toilets, no lights and even no windows. Definitely pay extra for the comfort of a better class, especially if you're travelling overnight. First- and second-class usually require advance booking. In Europe,

you'll be charged a supplement (around $10) for a seat reservation but this is worth it if the alternative is standing for six hours. Supplements also apply for faster trains and couchettes (seats that convert to bunks).
- In Asia, you'll encounter a bewildering array of bus services – several classes plus private and public services, or tourist and government buses. Some travellers have a great time on government buses in one country (Thailand), and then the bus-ride-from-hell experience in a neighbouring country (Vietnam). Ask tourism workers and fellow travellers about which is the best option in a particular country.
- For city travel, train tickets are bought at stations; bus and tram tickets can be bought from kiosks and newsstands. You can also purchase a ticket from the driver, although you could be charged more than for a pre-purchased ticket. Make sure you have small change.
- In countries where the transport system runs like clockwork, get there well before departure time, especially if you haven't reserved a seat. In developing countries, delays are inevitable,

so leave plenty of time for connections. It can still pay to get there early – some buses leave before the scheduled time if they fill quickly.
- Taxis in the developing world can be anything from a roaring motorcycle to a bicycle rickshaw. The fare is decided before the ride. Have some change on hand and some idea of what it should cost.
- Beware of mercenary taxi drivers, especially in tourist meccas like Europe, Egypt and Mexico. Make sure the cab has a meter. If not, look elsewhere. If the meter is 'broken' and you've arrived at 11 p.m. with no clue where you're spending the night, you might have to take your chances. But always agree on the fare before you get in the cab. If you've booked your accommodation, it's always a good idea to ask the hotel or a tourism worker how much a taxi ride from the airport or train/bus station should cost.
- At airports, don't head straight for the taxi rank. Major airports have a regular bus shuttle or train line to the centre of town, both of which are far cheaper than taxi. From Narita

Airport to the centre of Tokyo, even with an honest cabbie, you won't get much change from $400. The train costs about $60.

Travel passes

Buying a single ticket for each trip is rarely the cheapest way to get around. Consider a day pass if you're zipping around town on the metro – out sightseeing, back to the hotel, then out again in the evening. If you're spending a week in a major city such as London, Paris or Moscow and plan to spend four or five days moving around, a weekly pass will save you time and money. In some cities, you can buy three-day passes or multi-ticket books, which work out cheaper than buying individual tickets.

Many European cities have integrated transport systems, allowing you to ride on train, metro, tram and bus on the same ticket. Ask at tourist offices, public transport offices or train stations. All of these can sell daily or weekly passes and tell you about transfer options. Students, under 26s, seniors and families are usually eligible for discounts.

For the great bulk of tourists, 'travel pass' is synonymous with Eurail Pass. This is a ticket to ride the great rail networks of seventeen European countries (notable exceptions being Britain, Russia, the Czech Republic and Poland).

Eurail passes come in no less than nine varieties. The top-of-the-line Eurail Pass allows unlimited travel in all seventeen countries for periods of between fifteen days and three months. The cheapest ticket, the Eurail Saver Flexipass, buys you ten days of travel over two months. Visit **www.eurail.com** for all the dizzying options.

If Eurail is too extensive for your needs, consider a Europass, which covers less territory than the Eurail Pass. The five Europass countries are France, Germany, Italy, Spain and Switzerland, but you have the option of adding other countries (e.g. Greece) or groups of countries (e.g. Benelux). The Eurail web site (**www.eurail.com**) also covers Europass.

No matter what your travel plans in Europe, chances are there's a rail pass out there for you. Even if your travel is limited to one country, contact the national rail line and ask what specials are on offer. BritRail or Deutsche Bahn could save you a lot of money. Visit **www.raileurope.com**.

An easy trap is to design a travel itinerary around the pass, rather than choose the right pass for your trip. Many travellers stretch themselves too thin trying to ride every last dollar and kilometre of track out of the pass. They'll head up to Norway for a day because 'it's free' or already paid for. Or they'll spend just two days in Rome because otherwise they're 'wasting' travel time.

Study carefully the conditions and limitations of your pass. For faster trains, a supplement normally applies. If you're heading from Germany to Italy via Austria on a Europass, you'll have to fork out the regular fare for the swing through Austria (not a Europass country).

Beware of 'free' passage on ferry routes, especially the English Channel or between Italy and Greece. This will cost one day of travel on your Flexipass and perhaps plenty more in port and departure taxes, holiday supplements, overpriced onboard food and the like.

Yes, there really is public transport in LA

It's a central piece of LA lore: in this city of six-lane freeways and tangled overpasses, you're a slave to the automobile. You can't go anywhere in LA without a car. When we asked locals about transport options, responses ranged from: 'Don't even think of taking public transport' to 'What is public transport?' Like much about Los Angeles, popular perceptions are deceptive.

Naturally, we took the advice of locals. With baby in tow, we didn't want to find ourselves on a dark station platform kilometres from our hotel, waiting forty minutes for a weekend train. So from our hotel in Santa Monica we took a taxi to Hollywood, via an expensive detour through downtown. When we alighted at Hollywood Boulevard, we were lighter in the pockets by US$55. Many happy hours were then spent hoofing it along the Walk of Fame, Sunset Strip and Melrose Avenue into West Hollywood and then to Beverly Hills to smirk at high-maintenance poodles and people on Rodeo Drive.

Back on Santa Monica Boulevard, we were still sufficiently outraged by the taxi fare to actually consider walking the ten kilometres back to the beach. Just then a bus pulled up. Its sign read 'Santa Monica'. Too easy. Sure, we were surrounded by people who looked like they'd come from an audition for *Natural Born Killers 2*. But the ride back cost $4 – for two!

chapter 14: ACCOMMODATION

Pre-booking a place

Your style of accommodation and how to find it depends on several variables: where and when you go, the type of trip (long-haul backpacking or a secluded island retreat), and how important the accommodation is to your enjoyment of the destination. On many trips, it's a combination of pre-booking and finding places as you go.

Pre-booking provides certainty, saves time and allows you to budget for the exact amount of your stay. The downside is that it can be disappointing – you could be kilometres from the action. At worst, pre-booking can be an illuminating experience in the trickery of travel brochures. You may find yourself opening the door to a malodorous basement room with no natural light, a saggy bed, and walls reverberating to the doof-doof-doof of the techno dance club next door. So that's why the price was so good!

The longer the trip, the more likely you'll have to pre-book at least some of the accommodation. Booking is essential in major cities during peak times such as summer, Christmas–New Year and, needless to say, during major festivals and events.

Any special accommodation will require pre-booking – a maharaja's palace in India, a castle hostel in Germany, beach bures in Fiji, the picturesque *pensione* right off the town square, boat and train hotels. Island resorts mostly require booking – and their packages are often much better value than walking straight into the lobby.

The more important accommodation is to the enjoyment of a trip, the earlier you should start your search. There's little point staying in a beautiful walking city such as Prague if you're stuck in the outskirts and a long train ride from the best bits. Pay a little more if you want to be in the thick of it. This doesn't mean you should head for the nearest bland, multi-storey hotel; but finding affordable, atmospheric lodgings in a central location can take some creativity and effort.

Don't assume that reservations are only for fancy hotels. In Europe during the summer months, budget accommodation fills up fast, especially anything listed in a popular guidebook. Make your calls sooner rather than later.

Guidebooks, traveller recommendations and the Internet are all good sources of information for booking accommodation. National and regional tourist offices can let you in on special types of accommodation, such as castle hotels, farm stays and the like. At home, you can go through a travel agent or travel wholesaler. Although their listings can be pricier, you can be assured of a good standard as all hotels are screened.

Finding a place on arrival

Lining up accommodation as you go means you can shop around, save money and find exactly what you're after. But travelling like this means finding a bed will be a daily concern. For some, that's exciting; for others, unnerving. The daily hunt for a room could curtail many sightseeing trips. And of course you run the risk of seeing 'House Full' signs all over town and the prospect of sleeping in a train station.

Those taking this route should make use of guidebooks, recommendations from other travellers and information boards at airports, and train and bus stations. Backpacker and hostel associations are also helpful. In many cities, all a budget traveller needs to do is take a bus or taxi to backpacker-central and ask around.

Where they exist, tourist offices can be extremely helpful. They know what's out there and what it costs. They can throw up options (convents, student dorms) that you never knew were available, as well as act as a booking agency (often for a fee). Many tourist offices, however, do not have the cheapest places among their glossy brochures. If there's no tourist office and no listings in your guidebook, ask taxi drivers or fellow bus or train passengers about a good place to stay.

At many train and bus stations around the world, you could be accosted by locals (perhaps children in Africa) wanting to rent you private accommodation. This can range from delightful (a self-contained cottage in a lavender garden on an island in Croatia) – to depressing (a no-privacy room in a crumbling communist apartment block). The main complaint from travellers is that these places are far from the centre of town, despite the owners' inevitable 'ten minutes away' sales pitch. Be wary of their well-rehearsed patter. Pictures can be misleading. Dealing with the owner, especially if they happen to be a sweet old lady, is preferable to the bejewelled, mobile-phone-wielding agents. If you feel uncomfortable in this situation, say that you have accommodation lined up and head for a tourist office. They often also have private rooms on their books, or can refer you to an agency that specialises in private accommodation.

The best tip is to get into town early. The earlier you arrive, the more time you have to look and decide. When barrelling in late at night, sheer desperation could land you in a fleapit that you never would have taken if you had another option.

It's difficult to get the booking-versus-finding mix exactly right. You might find yourself turned away from the single hostel in a dreary burg that you never imagined would require a booking.

Or you could settle into your pre-booked room in a concrete box of a hotel, only to look across the street and see the perfect traditional guesthouse. Don't let it spoil your trip, though. Even veteran travellers don't get it right all the time.

What to look for

Seek out the type of accommodation that a particular place does 'best', such as B&Bs in rural Britain; *chambres d'hôte* in France; *pensioni* in Italy; chalet inns in Austria, Germany and Switzerland; *ryokan* in Japan; or beachside huts in Thailand. Smaller, family-run places tend to be friendlier and more atmospheric. If you're sticking to hostels, you'll have to expand your search in places without a long tradition of hostelling, such as Africa, Latin America and much of Asia. Usually, there is plentiful cheap accommodation in other guises. A guidebook will provide a run-down of all the options.

In the developing world, a few extra dollars could be the difference between a dorm bed down the hall from a dingy communal bathroom and a big, comfortable room with a balcony, private bath and sit-down toilet. A better room needn't blow your budget. Couples and groups can also get a better standard (and save money) by asking for double or triple rooms at hostels.

Put all timidity aside and ask to see the room. Assess its comfort, cleanliness, safety and convenience. Check the bed linen for age and whether it's been freshly laundered. Test the bed's firmness. You won't get a good sleep on a lumpy or sagging mattress. Check that the lights, heating or air-conditioning work. Dust and odours will give you a sense of a room's cleanliness. For safety, make sure that the windows open and that there is a smoke detector or fire escape. Also, check that the door locks securely from the inside. Finally, is the location quiet and convenient? Will you need earplugs to sleep with the roaring traffic outside your window? Is it worth paying more to be closer to the centre of town?

Ask to see a couple of rooms. Hotels rarely quote you the cheapest rooms in the hope that you'll pay more. Confirm if it's the cheapest room they have. Conversely, if you don't like the room you are shown, ask to see a better one.

If you're staying in a dorm room, check out the

communal bathroom. One glance here – specifically at the receptacle for used toiletpaper – will probably tell you all you need to know about the place's standards.

When you're quoted a price, ask if it includes breakfast, taxes, weekend supplements, mosquito nets and any other add-on you can possibly think of. Confirm whether the rate is per person or per room. Avoid nasty surprises at check-out time.

Depending on where you are and how full the place is, you may well be able to negotiate the price. Almost nobody pays rack rate. If you're staying more than a couple of days, especially in the low season, ask for a discount. To put it more subtly, ask if the rate you're given is the best they can do.

You should also ask whether communal bathrooms are open all day and hot water is available at all times. Some places only heat water in the mornings and evenings to save on power bills. At crowded hostels and guesthouses, unless you are quick off the mark, you could find yourself among the great unwashed. Even if you have a private bath, ask if you have hot water. In some places (e.g. Africa), the two don't always go together. Similarly, to reduce power costs, some places (e.g. in Greece) turn off the air-conditioning during the day. You could return from a day at the beach to a stifling box.

Don't take the first room you are shown, especially if you aren't happy with it. You have to shop around and compare in order to get an idea of the amenities your money can buy. While you do get what you pay for, in many cases you get a lot more if you're prepared to look harder. The list of what to be suspicious of is fairly long. Some things to look out for include:

- Cockroaches in the lobby – never a good sign! Ditto for porn magazines at reception. If you're unimpressed with the lobby or reception area, the rooms are unlikely to be an improvement.
- Heavily made-up ladies arriving and leaving by the hour. In parts of Africa, Asia, Latin America and Europe, many cheap hotels are also brothels. Not recommended for women travelling alone.
- Suspicious holes in the walls or ceiling (yes, peepholes for spying on guests).

- At check-in, be suspicious of any hotel that insists on holding your passport. This is fairly common in Vietnam, to ensure you pay your bill and in case police or other officials want to check your visa. Supply a photocopy but never hand over your passport. Unscrupulous operators could use it to extort money out of you or even sell it. Explain that you need your passport to cash traveller's cheques. Offer to pay a cash deposit instead – and make sure you get a receipt.
- Some hotels insist on guests leaving their room key at reception when going out. Although this is ostensibly so you cannot make copies of the key, it can be an irresistible temptation for unethical staff or owners. Try sneaking out with the key or see what happens if you threaten to take your business elsewhere.
- In poorer regions, hotel proprietors may ask for upfront payment each day. Only do this if you can get receipts.
- Look beyond the convenient location. Sometimes it's all a place has going for it. Airport hotels can be the worst in rip-off rates and sub-standard rooms as they know you're not staying

there for the ambience. While you shouldn't stay at a nicer place if it means possibly missing a flight, avoid this situation in towns by looking beyond the ordinary, overpriced hotels clustered around train and bus stations.
- Beware of taxi drivers who insist on taking you to the 'best', most centrally located hotel. They could be getting kickbacks to deposit travellers there. If you do ask a taxi driver for a place to stay, make clear your expectations and price limit.
- Beware of establishments named after well-known landmarks or famous natives. In Austria, for example, anything with Mozart or Amadeus in the name is likely to be a rip-off.

Sometimes you just don't know what you'll get, so don't be too hard on yourself if you pay $90 for a decent room and still get bed-bugs.

chapter 15: SHOPPING

What you can bring back to Australia

See the Australian Customs brochure 'Know Before You Go' for extensive information on what you can and can't bring into Australia. Call 1300 363 263 from within Australia or visit **www.customs.gov.au**.

If you intend to buy a car, yacht or other craft on your trip, contact Customs before you leave to check the requirements. The import or export of more than A$10 000 in cash (in any currency) also must be reported. If this situation could apply to you, contact the Australian Transaction Reports and Analysis Centre on 1800 021 037.

The duty-free allowance for Australians returning home is:

- A$400 worth of goods, not including alcohol or tobacco. Gifts bought for or by you count as part of this allowance.
- 1.125 litres of alcoholic liquor.
- 250 cigarettes, or 250 grams of cigars or tobacco product.
- Unlimited personal items, such as clothes and products for personal hygiene or grooming.
- Personal items (e.g. a laptop computer) owned and used by you for over twelve months.

Members of the same family can combine their allowances. Anything above and beyond this should be declared. Stiff penalties apply for evading duties and tax.

Sending bulky things home

You've just bought a rich Turkish carpet that will look magnificent in your study . . . Now – how do you get it back home? Fortunately, there are companies who can ship home your prize purchases. The main options are post offices, shipping companies and international couriers. The latter is the most expensive, but also the most reliable for urgent or valuable items. Post offices can send items airmail (often prohibitively expensive) or surface mail (combined air and sea). Sea mail is considerably cheaper but slower and less reliable. For large and heavy items such as rugs, shipping companies are the best option as they charge by space, rather than weight. The delivery could be to your door, or you might have to collect it from a port facility, after paying import duties.

For Australians, shipping anything is rarely cheap. You could spend $15 on a Malawi chair and pay ten times that to fly it home. But it's worth it to know your treasured mementos will get home in one piece.

Backpacker ghettos are the place to start your inquiries. They're crammed with price-conscious businesses and services – post offices, travel companies, and so on – who can handle your request or point you to someone who can. Also ask other travellers in Internet cafés, at your guesthouse, etc.

Bargaining

Get a sense of what the real prices are by looking around shops and markets and asking hotel staff and other travellers. As a general rule, you should pay about half the original asking price. Bargaining is widespread in Africa, Latin America and Asia (except for Japan, Korea and Taiwan). Don't be embarrassed to haggle – it's expected. In some places (especially Arab countries such as Egypt and Morocco), bargaining is a sport and vendors will be disappointed if you don't play the game.

Treat bargaining as a social, not just a commercial, interaction. When buying carpets in Morocco, for example, you will be seated, have every rug rolled out for your inspection, served endless mint teas, treated like royalty, and finally beaten down to your half-price rule. This may still be 50 per cent more than rock-bottom price, but it's a memory you'll have forever.

If you've been ripped off

Never pay more than you intended. Decide what something is worth to you, set a sale price and don't go beyond it. Don't assume you've been ripped off simply because you paid more than the locals. In many places, there is a local price and a tourist price and never the twain shall meet. It's insulting and embarrassing to see affluent

Westerners haggle over five cents in a flea market.

If you suspect you've been fleeced, ask other travellers, especially those who've been on the road for longer, what the item should cost. In most cases, the difference in Australian money is negligible. Take it as a learning experience or as a contribution to the local economy. Your best protection against rip-off merchants is to have a clear idea of an item's worth. If the opening price is ten times what you're prepared to pay, just walk away.

chapter 16: TRAVELLING WITH OTHERS

Groups

Travelling with a group of friends is a great way to get the best rooms at hostels and guesthouses, as well as save on hire cars, taxis and laundry. It can open up some options – for example, boat hire, camping – that you wouldn't or couldn't do on your own. The language barrier is a lot less formidable if you can talk to and rely on the linguistic skills of others, and there's safety in numbers, too.

But travelling in a group can require a major attitude adjustment, especially for individuals who like to take charge and make decisions. The major decisions – what to do, where to stay – should be taken collectively. Limit the group to four people or less. Any bigger and it becomes impossible to balance competing interests and keep everyone happy.

The one big disadvantage of group travel is less time for individual interests and pursuits, so set aside time in the itinerary for people to do their own thing. This will help ease the feeling that you're on *their* holiday, rather than your own. Going separate ways for a while also makes it easier to meet locals, as groups tend to be insular.

Organised tours

Some independent travellers wouldn't be caught dead in a tour group. Their loss. Tours can range from multi-country romps through Europe to safaris in East Africa, to two-hour city walking tours. They can be totally structured or a flexible, self-guided itinerary. Plenty of tour operators can show you a wonderful time, provided you choose a tour that truly reflects your interests. In some places (e.g. the Amazon), an organised tour is pretty much the only way you'll get access.

Tours can be as sedate or as adventurous as you

like. Many tours are thoughtfully put together, show great sensitivity for local cultures and provide lasting experiences and memories.

Many travellers get the best of both worlds by taking a tour at the beginning of a trip before venturing out on their own. This is an especially appealing option for young and first-time travellers.

The advantage of organised tours is that everything is arranged and you won't be sweating on train tickets or restaurant reservations. Structure is also their weak point: you can't stay longer in places that really grab you, and you can feel like part of a herd because you're not engaging with the culture on your own. Try to arrange a few days either side of the tour to explore alone. Organised tours are also invariably more expensive than DIY trips.

Ask a travel agent about tours that interest you. If they can't book it themselves, they can direct you to someone who can. The travel sections of metropolitan newspapers can unearth some interesting tours. Also try national and regional tourist offices and web sites such as **www.specialtytravel.com**. Or search the Internet for areas of special interest, such as birdwatching, religious tours, Eastern Europe, etc.

Children

Travelling with kids is both wonderfully rewarding and bloody hard work. Children often make great travellers and it's the parents who end up exhausted. This is because travelling with kids requires the same level of organisation as an invasion of Europe. The smaller the child, the more preparation required. On the plus side, you will be welcomed by locals wherever you go and people will go out of their way to be helpful. A child is the best ice-breaker.

Airlines can be terrifically helpful, but you need to alert them to your needs well before you fly. Ask for a skycot (if your child meets the weight restriction). These are located in the first row (bulkhead) of each section. Even if your child is too big for the cot, request the bulkhead seats because there is more wriggle room for kids and they can't bother passengers in front. Also, these seats offer uninterrupted movie viewing and they're close to the galley at eating times and the storage cupboard where prams are stowed. Airlines will tell you at check-in whether your pram/stroller can go as onboard luggage – this depends on the aircraft's storage capacity and the size of your baby carriage.

Some airlines (like the kid-friendly Qantas) will supply nappies, a change mat and a change tray in the bathroom as well as commercial baby food, bibs, books and activities. However, you should bring your own supplies, especially if your child is a fussy eater (aren't they all?). Airlines do not supply formula and although it may be readily available at your destination, it could be very different from the brand your child is used to.

Travelling with small children virtually rules out hostels, guesthouses and B&Bs as accommodation options. You'll probably need your own bathroom and possibly kitchen facilities. This means you're looking at more expensive accommodation but the amenities and peace of mind will be worth it. Bring a favourite toy, pillow or blanket to help kids settle into strange beds. A bath book can coax them into strange tubs.

Big rooms are essential for toddlers and restless preschoolers. Ask to see the room; even some two-bedroom units are very cramped, without room to swing a cat. Check the thickness of the walls. If they're tissue-thin, other guests could complain about the noise level in your room. Go elsewhere or ask to be away from other guests.

Eating options are also more limited with kids. Many children don't go for rich restaurant food (even if many places offer a kids' menu), so you'll be doing more self-catering, between the inevitable meals at McDonalds!

Staying by the beach means plenty of recreational space for kids. Otherwise, you'll need to seek out parks and playgrounds. Luckily, this isn't difficult. A frisbee, ball or simple kite will keep them amused and encourage interaction with other children.

Kids act as a natural brake on hectic itineraries. You simply can't go from a church to an art gallery to dinner to the opera. Remember to include places the kids will enjoy – such as a zoo, aquarium, interactive science centre, toy or doll museum, or puppet show. If children are old enough, give them a guidebook or some options and let them decide. Kids will be more enthusiastic about the day's activities if they helped plan them.

Wherever you go, be prepared for your child to be showered with sweets, balloons, small toys and attention from locals. Parents can be inundated with questions and compliments. It's an easy way to fall into conversation with locals.

TOP 10 TRAVEL TIPS

What better way to blow your money and time than on travel? With a bit of planning, you can help ensure that you'll spend that time and money well, and remember your trip for all the right reasons.

You don't have to plan every last detail, but the most important points to consider before you leave home are as follows.

1. Research your destination. Its laws, local customs, climate and natural environment will shape your travel plans.
2. Consider the worst-case scenario when taking out travel insurance. This is what your policy should provide cover for.
3. Pre-book some accommodation, especially for the first night or two.

4. Avoid an overly ambitious itinerary. You can always do more at your destination if you feel up to it.
5. Travel light. It's much easier to acquire what you need, rather than off-load what you don't.
6. Learn some greetings and useful phrases in the local language. At least bring a phrasebook for emergencies.
7. Have some contingency plans for theft or loss of your travel documents and money.
8. Keep in touch with regular phone calls, faxes or emails, especially if you're heading into remote regions. Give people locally or at home an idea of when you expect to return.
9. Wear culturally appropriate attire. Dress presentably when dealing with officials.
10. Don't worry if every detail of your trip does not go according to plan. The unpredictability of travel is a big part of its allure.

We leave the best tip and last word to Confucius: 'Wheresoever you go, go with all your heart.'